AL DETTER

Mishaps, Mistakes, and Mischief

SKELLIG PRESS

This book is lovingly dedicated to
Marie, my dear wife of more than fifty years.

Our tears, they were many
Our laughter was more.

Contents

II   Humorous Stories From My Ministry

III   Overheard

Foreword

The Bible speaks multiple times about the benefit of laughter for the human soul. Counselors and therapists will also tell you that a good sense of humor is essential for a successful and happy life.

When eHarmony recently did a study on humor in their effort to make "good romantic matches," they identified nine different categories of humor:

- Physical (as in slapstick)
- Wit and Wordplay (including puns)
- Self-Deprecating
- Surreal (think Monty Python)
- Improvisational
- Topical
- Observational
- Bodily Functions (you know the type!)
- Dark

According to their poll, physical humor is the most popular, and dark humor the least. The other types fall somewhere in between.

While a fairly good list, I don't think it's comprehensive enough. To their list I would add situational humor. Sometimes you just find yourself in an awkward or humorous situation. It's not observational because you're right in the middle of it! And it may not be physical.

I would also add laughter that's related to a sense of joy and wonder, and often – relief. Aren't we all touched at times by something amazing or poignant or heart-rending, and the only appropriate response is laughter?

Does God have a sense of humor? It's been said that no one who looks at His creation could think otherwise! Elephants and giraffes and – ahem – *humans* are often cited as examples. God begins with each individual, giving him or her a unique personality, full of odd quirks and conflicting traits that are sure to lead to humorous situations. Then He places each individual into a "family of origin" to interact with others who have interesting personalities and quirks before launching them into the broader world – where the humorous situations expand exponentially!

Like a river of living water, humor and laughter have flowed through my life from the beginning, washing away sorrow, helping me through rough patches, and watering the seeds of love and friendship, causing them to grow stronger. Some of that water flows in this book.

I believe you will find most of the aforementioned types of humor (except surreal and dark) represented in the following pages.

Enjoy!

Cindy Hogg, Editor

Preface

THE LAUGHTER BOX

If I knew the box where laughter was kept,
No matter how large the key
Or strong the bolt, I would try so hard
'Twould open, I know, for me.
Then over the land and sea broadcast,
I'd scatter the laughter to play,
So that careworn people might hold it fast
For many and many a day.

If I knew a box that was large enough
To hold all the frowns I meet,
I would like to gather them, everyone,
From nursery, school, and street.
Then folding and holding, I'd pack them in,
And turning the monster key,
I'd hire a giant to drop the box
To the depths of the deep, deep sea.

– Maud Wyman, The Sacred Heart Review, Volume 51, Number 17, April 11, 1914, adapted

I've always wanted to write several published books. It never happened until now. When I've been to libraries, bookstores, and large used book sales at which there were multiplied thousands of volumes, I'd think to myself, *If there are this many authors in the world, why am I not one of them? Certainly, I can't be that unqualified and lacking in brain power.* I never got beyond that question.

It wasn't for lack of ideas. In my files are dozens of topics I'd like to write on. Brian Kelly, a pastor friend of mine, told me to set aside Thursday mornings to write. I never did.

There's a plethora of Christian books on the market by accomplished authors. They make profound contributions - from leadership to theology to spirituality to finances to families. Surely, any book I'd write would be a serious and helpful book like that.

Wrong.

My first book is a book on humor – dozens of funny stories from my personal life and ministry. The reason for a book like this? This world is a tough place. There's heartache, tragedy, disease, war, disappointment, anxiety, difficulties, political wrangling, and heaviness wherever you turn – in families, in churches, at work, and in life in general. People need to laugh.

Even the writers of the Bible understood this:

- Job 8:21 - "He will yet fill your mouth with laughter, and your lips with shouting."
- Proverbs 15:13 - "A glad heart makes a cheerful face, but by sorrow of heart the spirit is crushed."
- Proverbs 17:22 - "A joyful heart is good medicine, but a crushed spirit dries up the bones."
- Ecclesiastes 3:4 - "A time to weep, and a time to laugh, a time to mourn, and a time to dance."

Richard Baxter, a 17th Century English Puritan church leader and theologian, had a contrarian opinion about humor. In his classic book, *The Reformed Pastor*, he enjoins pastors: *Oh, speak not one cold or careless word about so great a business as heaven or hell! Whatever you do, let the people see that you are in good earnest.*

Truly, brethren, there are great works that are to be done, and you must not think that trifling will dispatch them. You cannot break men's hearts by jesting with them or telling a smooth tale. Men will not cast away their dearest pleasures upon a drowsy request of one that seemeth not to mean as he speaks... (London: James Nisbet and Co., 1860, pp. 312-313).

I understand Baxter's intent. But I respectfully contend that we were made to laugh, to do something that animals can't do. Humor is part of the image of God.

Laughter produces emotional healing and promotes joy. It helps to cement relationships, including among the saints of the church. Even in preaching, laughter helps the medicine go down.

An article in *Psychology Today* says that the average four-year-old laughs 300 times a day. The average 40-year-old? Only four ("You're Not Laughing Enough, and That's No Joke," *psychology.com*, posted June 21, 2011). Other blogs on the topic have cited 15-20 as the average number of daily laughs for adults. I hope this book will increase your frequency.

A big thanks to all the people mentioned in this book, over 175 of them. (In some cases, I've left names out or used aliases for sensitivity reasons.) Without them, life would have been far too serious. They've helped others and me to laugh, and to laugh often over the years.

Add a big thanks to Edoardo Albert, a new friend and accomplished author, who nudged and coached me when I got stuck on this project. And to Cindy Hogg who took an explosion of words and stories and helped fashion them into something shorter and worthy of reading.

A big thanks to Danielle Hartland who designed the book cover. And finally, to my wife Marie and my son Jared for meticulously reading and proofing the manuscript in preparation for publication.

The stories in this book span nearly sixty years. They're autobiographical in nature. I've tried to be as accurate in recollection as possible. There may be some holes or inaccuracies here and there, but the stories are substantially on target.

As I reflected on my life for this book, I noticed that I laughed more as a younger person. I'm realizing that I need to laugh more as I age, and that it's important to hang around happy people as much as possible.

Life can wear you down, and you can lose your laughing edge. Maybe that's why this quote from Senator Alan Simpson's eulogy at George H. W. Bush's funeral caught my attention, "Humor is the universal solvent against the abrasive elements of life." This world needs a lot of solvent.

A word of caution. I tell some stories that contain some earthy material, which may be surprising for a preacher. But in this book, I'm a person first, a preacher second. Yet as a preacher, I couldn't avoid including a few spiritual nuggets along the way.

Years ago, country singer Buck Owens sang a song called, *Crying Time*. As you read this book, it's "laughing time."

*The Scripture references above are from the English Standard Version.

I

Humorous Stories From My Life

1

A SHY ROMANTIC

My mother had a rule for my sister and me – no dating until we were sixteen. That was okay because, as a young boy, I was extremely bashful around pretty girls. But as I ventured into my teen years, I thought it time to test the boundaries.

Janet Adie was a neighbor girl across the street from our back alley. She was also in my grade at school. We got along really well, as all the kids in the neighborhood hung out together. The net result? I developed a secret crush on her.

The day I turned 15, I thought, *Enough of this shyness. I'm old enough to date. If I ask Janet out, Mom will be sure to understand.* My plan was to ask her to go to a movie with me in our hometown. It was within easy walking distance, and all the kids in town went on dates to the Broad Theater. I asked, and she accepted.

The day before the date, I told my mom. It was like the law of the Medes and Persians. Mom wouldn't bend. Her edict was etched in stone. There'd be no date at 15! I was to march over to Janet's house and let her know – right then!

That was the longest walk I ever took. Out my back yard. A turn to the right into the alley. Across the street and straight ahead to her apartment door. It was a second-floor apartment and the dimly-lit steps looked a mile high as I began to ascend them.

Trembling, I knocked on the door and, after what seemed like an eternity, she opened it. With quavering voice, I explained the situation the best I could without throwing my mother under the bus. Janet smiled, patted me on the shoulder, and said, "That's okay." We never did go out on a date. The "Janet" experience only multiplied my shyness.

Sixteen came and with it my driver's license. It was time to obey my mother's rule!

There was only one car in our family, but Mom and Dad were most generous in letting me use it for dating on weekends. Incredibly, this shy guy used the car quite a lot. I went steady with two girls during high school – not at the same time, of course! But in both cases, I had a shyness regression. Here's why.

My first steady went to our church. She was very active there, and the church was our second home. I'd never kissed a girl before, and we dated for months just holding hands. One Sunday night, I decided to kiss her goodnight. I was nervous all evening.

I pulled into her driveway and turned off the engine. I looked her in the eyes and leaned towards her. She knew a kiss was coming, so she stopped my approach. What she said next, I'll never forget.

"You can't kiss me. My mom told me that's how you get pregnant." I felt totally shocked and embarrassed. I swallowed hard, mumbled an apology, escorted her to her door, and hurried home. We continued to date but I never kissed her, not after what she said.

She faded from the picture and I began to go steady with another girl from a different church. I liked her a lot but was very reluctant to show any affection. My shy nature accompanied by that kiss shut-down from the previous girl did me in. I was reluctant to even hold her hand.

One night I took her to dinner. In those days, there were front bench seats in cars. The question for guys when they'd pick up their date was

4

always, *Will she slide by my side in the middle of the seat or stay over by the door on the passenger side?* If the latter were true, she'd be known by the letters "DDH," which meant "Darned Door Hugger." My date slid over to my side and a good feeling came over me.

After dinner, we headed toward her house, miles away. She sat next to me again, but I couldn't get the courage to hold her hand. I started a count-down and said to myself, *When I pass the next twenty telephone poles, I'll hold her hand.* Twenty poles came and went and I'd repeat the goal. We were almost to her house when it was now or never. I finally took her hand! She accepted it, to my joy and relief.

My best friend Vern Gahman started to date Connie Price, the girl he'd eventually marry. We talked about our romantic experiences, because we shared everything. Kissing was a regular part of their relationship. I still had never kissed a girl, and he told me that it was about time.

Vern and I both wore glasses. He said, "You really can't kiss well with your glasses on. You need to take them off." Those words stayed in the back of my mind.

Soon the night came when I decided to kiss my new girlfriend. We were sitting on her couch. I leaned toward her. She leaned toward me. Our lips met and we embraced. I had a breakthrough!

Then the words of my friend came to mind: *You can't kiss very well with your glasses on.* So while I was kissing her, I reached up with my left hand to behind my left ear and began to nudge my glasses away from my face. I continued to embrace her with my right arm. With a little awkward finagling, my glasses finally fell to the sofa.

I could tell she wasn't thrilled with that maneuver and the next thing she said was, "I think it's time for you to leave." I believe I freaked her out, and it was all my friend's fault. I never kissed her after that, and my glasses never came off again. I headed off to college, and she met someone else.

And so it was that I only ever kissed one girl besides my mother, sister, and other female relatives. And then I met Marie, my future wife. I kissed her for the first time on Memorial Day, 1969, on the shores of Lake Michigan in Chicago. It was a beautiful kiss, and she returned it.

And the glasses thing? I didn't have to worry because, by then, I no longer wore them. Marie and I have been kissing every day ever since. She finally cured me of my shyness.

2

THE SWEATERS

When you're in high school, you think those are the main people you'll know the rest of your life. College proves you wrong. New lifetime friends emerge from everywhere.

I'm from a small town in Southeastern Pennsylvania – Souderton. It's my assumption that most people have never heard of the place. I'm usually right.

It was my freshman year at the Moody Bible Institute in Chicago, and I was meeting people by the truckload. I tried to capture names and where people were from. When I heard that Dave Landis and Mitch Nase were from Quakertown and Boyertown respectively, I paid particular attention. Those towns were close to Souderton!

Here we were, meeting for the first time at college and all the while, we grew up perhaps fifteen miles apart. And Dave? He worked right up the road from where I worked while we went to our respective high schools. I could see Cassel's Produce, and he could see Acme Supermarkets, yet we had never met. We became instant friends 800 miles from home.

We all liked to sing. I joined the Moody Chorale. Dave and Mitch roomed together, and they joined the Men's Glee Club. Living in the same dorm, it wasn't long until we'd get together and sing familiar gospel and folk songs in rich three-part harmony. Mitch and I played guitar. Soon we realized we had a good-sounding trio. We discovered that we sounded particularly good in the echoey basement stairwells of the Institute's Torrey-Gray Auditorium where we practiced.

Our freshman class was getting to know each other. It was accelerated by class mixers. The organizers were always looking for talent, so we volunteered.

We made our freshman debut to great applause and decided to continue singing wherever we could find an engagement. We kidded each other about having a bus and going on tour. Our repertoire was developing and all we needed to really establish ourselves was a name for our group and matching outfits.

The name came easy. The clothes were another story.

In the 1960s, there was a secular music group called "The Dave Mitchell Trio." That was it! If we put our first names together, our group's name would have a familiar ring to it. How clever: *The DaveMitchAl Trio*. It was cheesy but no one ever clued us in.

The Smothers Brothers comedy duo was big back then. Dave and I had memorized one or two of their complete albums. We were quick-witted so, during our concerts, Dave would take the role of Tommy and I the role of Dick. We'd banter back and forth. One of our favorite Tommy lines was, "Mom always liked you best."

But we had yet to buy our matching clothes. That would take money.

Mohair cardigans were a hot item and we wanted to appear in style. One day we boarded the Chicago subway for the downtown Loop to browse the Marshall Field's as well as the Carson, Pirie, Scott department stores in search of mohair sweaters. We found some, but they were far too expensive for our limited college budgets.

A few days later, while walking on Dearborn Avenue, Dave and I saw a navy-blue mohair sweater in the window of a small men's apparel shop. It was perfect. As we entered the shop, we noticed a little old man sitting behind a sales counter. We asked about the blue sweater in the window. He looked at us strangely and said nothing.

Suddenly, a huge man appeared from a door behind the counter and asked if he could help us.

"We sing in a men's trio. We'd like three sweaters like the one in the window." They looked at us with surprise, but the big guy quoted us a price much lower than the prices downtown. It was an offer we couldn't refuse.

"We only have one," he said. "The one in the window, but it's not for sale."

"Can you order us three?" we replied, and he assured us they'd be there the following week. We didn't want to lose the sweaters so we each put down a small deposit. Those sweaters were sure to help establish our identity as a trio.

The next day, Dave spied the Chicago Tribune on a chair in the men's lobby on campus and couldn't believe his eyes. He took off running to find Mitch and me. We got the shock of our early college lives. On the front page was a picture of the big man who sold us the sweaters!

We couldn't read the story fast enough. The police had escorted him in handcuffs to the city jail. Turns out that the store was a front for the near Northside mafia operations. Our immediate response was, "Is the store still open? If it is, would it be safe to go there again?" And, "Will we lose our precious deposits?"

The next week finally came and we mustered the courage to return to the store. It was open! The little man was behind the counter. He had a package. In it were three sweaters. We breathed a huge sigh of relief and fumbled our way to our wallets. We paid the balance and got out of there as quickly as we could.

Back to the newspaper story. The big guy in the picture was the bouncer who screened the people who were allowed to enter the gambling "backroom." The police had been watching that location for quite some time, taking photos of people entering and leaving the store. The password for entry into the backroom? The blue sweater in the window!

The odds!

We don't know if the police ever took our pictures and we never got to the backroom. But those sweaters became the best conversation pieces a trio could ever have!

3

THE SHOWER

During my freshman year at the Moody Bible Institute in Chicago, many guys in my class lived in an old three-story dormitory affectionately called Ransom Hall. How old was it? So old that it was scheduled for demolition the following year.

Our dorm rooms had sinks. The toilets and showers were strategically placed in several spots along the dorm hallways. My room happened to be right across from one of these bathrooms. All I had to do was open my door and directly in front of me was the door to the facilities. So convenient!

One of my new friends, David Nicholes, lived several rooms down the hall to my left. Occasionally, we'd play a trick on one another. Nothing mean and nasty, just something pranky and inconvenient. Most guys on campus did it. We were no exceptions.

One lazy Saturday afternoon, the bathroom facility directly across from my room was in use and I could hear someone in the shower. I had no idea who it was. At that point, it was irrelevant because I was heading down the hall to chat with David.

When I got to his room, his door was open, but he was nowhere in sight. The bar of soap and a towel were gone from his sink area. I put two-and-two together and a light bulb went on in my brain: *it has to be David in the shower.*

Suddenly I was overcome with a mischievous spirit. I spied the wooden chair resting neatly in the opening of his study desk. It was a standard, wooden, library-type chair with no upholstery, but comfortable enough for long sessions of study. We all had identical ones in our dorm rooms.

I grabbed the chair and started down the hall. Destination? The bathroom door. I tilted the chair on its back legs, placing the top securely under the doorknob. It was a perfect fit. And the way I tilted it, engaging the doorknob and wedging it against the floor, it would be a chore for David to open the door.

I retreated to my room directly across from the action to listen for the battle that was about to ensue. I wasn't disappointed. Soon I heard rattling and banging and grunting and clanging until David finally worked the door open, muttering as he labored.

An unusual noise followed. It was the shower running full bore with the bathroom door wide open. Strange indeed. How could anyone else get in the shower that fast? And who would leave the door open?

Suddenly I heard a forlorn scream from down the hall, "Oh no! Don't tell me!" Understand, when David finally got the door open and saw the wooden chair that had restricted him, he assumed, *This has to be Al's chair. I'll show him. I'm going to soak his chair in the shower. The score will then be even.*

Into the shower went the chair.

But when David got to his room, towel around his waist and soap in hand, he noticed something very important missing – *his* chair. Suddenly he knew what had happened. He had soaked his own chair! This revelation had elicited his victim outburst.

Sometimes practical jokes go awry. Sometimes they go better than planned. This was one of those better occasions. David retrieved his soaked chair and was a good sport about it.

I laughed myself to sleep that night, my prank having exceeded all expectations. By bedtime, David was laughing, too.

4

THE TRENCH COAT

While in college, Moody Church in Chicago was my church of choice for Sunday evening services. It wasn't unusual to go as a little group of students or, if lucky enough, to take a date.

One Sunday evening my good friend, David Nicholes, had an informal date. I didn't, and none of my other friends were available to go with me.

I like to be around people, and I like a good church service, I said to myself. *It's off to "historic Moody Church."* Pastor George Sweeting liked to use that phrase a lot. The weather was rainy and blustery, but I still decided to embark on the mile-long walk from the Moody Bible Institute campus to the church.

When I arrived, I scoped out the expansive, nearly 4000-seat auditorium. (These were old wooden theater-style seats.) As I panned the crowd, I saw David and his date sitting in the middle of the sanctuary. I spied some open seats directly behind them, so I made my way there. In front of me was an empty seat. Directly to the left of that sat an older gentleman all by himself. Directly to the right of the empty seat sat David and his date.

14

The cold and drizzly night called for trench coats for the guys. A trench coat was nestled neatly in the empty seat directly in front of me, between David and the stranger.

As the service began, the immense pipe organ enhanced the festive gospel singing by the crowd. Then renowned musician Bill Pearce sang a solo and, for good measure, played his incredible trombone at intervals during his song. After the offering, we all stood and sang one more congregational song before the sermon.

Something came over me during that song. I thought, *Pick up David's trench coat and lay it on his seat.* Without anyone observing me, I quickly accomplished my mission.

We concluded the song, and we all sat down. To my amazement, David sat on the coat and didn't remove it. He continued to sit on that coat throughout the entire sermon.

My thoughts were as follows. *Okay, David. If you want to sit on your coat and permanently press it with wrinkles, it's your coat.*

Having seen me sitting behind him, David's thoughts were, *If Al is stupid enough to put his coat on my seat, I'm going to sit on it.*

Pastor Sweeting concluded his sermon, and we all stood for the final song. Then came the benediction. The service being over, the older gentlemen reached for his coat. It wasn't there. It was in David's seat!

The surprised man reached across the empty seat and picked up his coat. It was stuck in a tight, wrinkled ball as he lifted it upward. The man's and David's eyes met. Suddenly, David realized that it was not my coat. It was the stranger's coat! The embarrassing jolt of surprise that registered on David's face was priceless. So was the confused and incredulous expression on the old man's face.

And me? I was out of there in a flash with a laughing fit that almost debilitated me. Out the church door I went for the brisk walk back to campus. I left David to face the music.

About an hour later came a knock on my dorm door. *I wonder who that is,* I thought, knowing full well who it would be.

"Come in, David!"

He wasn't too excited about the recent proceedings. But as we debriefed and both came to the realization that he thought it was my coat and I thought it was his, we could hardly restrain our laughter.

The man left the church in bewilderment. David left the church knowing that he'd been had. And I left in laughter at the risk of a friendship. To this day, David and I still laugh and wonder if the man ever figured out what happened, and if he ever got the wrinkles out of his coat.

Postscript:

I sent this story to David for his review. The following is his response:

Dear Al,

Oh, my goodness! I'm suddenly feeling the bewildered embarrassment all over again as I desperately looked all over the church, especially the exits, for the one I knew was guilty but was nowhere in sight. With no evidence in hand to prove my innocence, I have no recollection of what lame excuse and apology I must have grasped for.

With time as a healer of such "loving" abuse, I've been laughing over and over since reading your story and the totally unexpected recall this afternoon of that cold Moody Church night.

I can still vividly see that tan trench coat like it was yesterday, laying totally misshapen and perfectly crushed in my seat. It was crumpled to such a degree that I wondered if even a hot iron could ever "put Humpty Dumpty together again." I really thought I had gotten you GOOD and was gloating big time that I had finally caught you off guard. Boy, was that ever a short-lived thought!

There, I'm laughing again. My only sense of relief is the fact that the older gentleman must have long ago gone to heaven where there are no tears and no bad memories of wrinkled coats.

It's a great story and it reminds me that you have a devious side that brought us and others to great laughter many times at Moody. Sometimes we were just laughing at how tickled you got when you pulled a really good one on someone. Somehow, I think that young college boy is still scheming today!!

"Thanks for the memories," as Bob Hope used to say. I've thoroughly enjoyed this one.

David

5

THE BLIND DATE

I hate to admit it, but when I went off to college, I'd never done laundry before. I came from the old Pennsylvania Dutch school of things: Mondays were laundry day, Tuesdays were ironing day, Wednesdays were mending day, Thursdays were cleaning day, and Fridays were baking day. And the mothers of the house? They did it all for the family.

As I packed my things to start college in Chicago, my mom gave me a crash course on washing clothes as she outfitted me with instructions, detergent, and a sack for dirty laundry. Using the dorm washing machines turned out to be easier than I expected. But I'd wait until I was down to my last items of clean clothes.

One problem was that some things, like dress pants and sports coats, needed to be dry-cleaned. Fortunately, on campus there was a dry cleaning "dry store" on the second floor above the Sweet Shop. (At a dry store you take your clothes to the shop, they're sent to a cleaners, and upon return, the clean clothes are staged in the shop for customer pickup.)

As school began in the fall of my freshman year, I bounded up the stairs to the cleaners with my dry cleaning. To my surprise, the store was closed. The school itself didn't operate it. It was a student venture and no student had come forward to run it.

A business opportunity! I thought. Always on the lookout for a bargain or way to earn some money, I made my way immediately to the Dean of Students' office, dirty clothes in hand. Dean Mohline was in and beckoned me to have a seat. He explained that the guy who previously ran the shop had graduated and no one else had stepped up to open it again.

I invented a business plan on the spot and made a proposal to the Dean. "I'd love to run that shop. Here's what I'd do," and I spun out my vision for its success. "What do you say?"

I walked out of his office the new "owner" of the store. I contacted a dry-cleaning business and made an agreement for pickup and delivery twice a week. I advertised through every means I could find on campus and, even though I was only open for four hours each weekday afternoon, I was soon flooded with business.

Money is a scarce commodity for college students. I made a little money off the cleaners, but I wanted to make more. *Why not make the cleaners a place where students could buy other products?* I mused. So I added things like hair spray, combs, brushes, nylon stockings, laundry detergent, and candy bars.

Instant success. My modest earnings increased, and Campus Cleaners became a one-stop shop for students and faculty alike. In fact, it became a place for people to hang out and chat.

College campuses are dating factories. For some students, dating comes easily. Romance begins and all goes well. For others, try as they may, successful dating eludes them. Many won't admit it, but they live with disappointment and self-doubt, especially when they go for weeks or longer without a date.

My entrepreneurial mind went to work, and I added another line to my services at the cleaners – a blind dating service. Yes indeed, a blind dating service. And it would be free. I figured that people would come to my shop to sign up for a date and they'd want to be sure they looked good. So naturally, they'd use my cleaners for coats and slacks and shirts and skirts and sweaters and my line of products.

I advertised the dating service on campus. It created a buzz. But would people come? Would shy people be that bold?

I worked out a discreet and confidential plan. I made a list of eligible male and female students. I'd be the middleman. If someone wanted a date, they'd come to my shop, tell me their story, and I'd make what I thought to be a decent match. And then I'd approach someone on my list and ask them if they'd be interested in a blind date. I mean, I was the precursor to Match.com!

Business wasn't brisk, but I was launching two to three dates a weekend. Surprisingly, some single faculty and staff got interested and began to use my service.

One day Bob Iler, a faculty member in his thirties, and an Institute employee in her late twenties, appeared on my radar. I made the arrangements. The date happened on a weekend. I couldn't wait until the following Monday to find out how things went.

They enjoyed themselves as much as one can on a first blind date. After dinner, they decided to take a walk down Michigan Avenue – "The Magnificent Mile." When they got to the base of the Wrigley Building, a robust gust of wind assailed them and out popped one of the lady's contact lenses.

What are the chances of finding a contact lens on the sidewalk, at night under a streetlight, on Michigan Avenue? But everyone knows that you give it the old college try, especially on a blind date.

Down on all fours went Bob as he patted his hands on the concrete sidewalk, trying to locate the proverbial needle in the haystack. Before long, his date was down on all fours as well, doing the same thing.

Here they were, two adults on a blind date – one adult now literally half-blind – crawling around on their hands and knees like toddlers on a sidewalk in the heart of a big city.

I don't remember if they ever found the lens. But the scene struck them as intensely funny. They could hardly control their laughter.

Alas, there was no second date for them. But for years afterward, each of them would remind me of the time they crawled around Chicago on their literal "blind date." The faculty member? He never married. The staff lady? She eventually met a wonderful man and has been happily married for years.

There's a prophetic irony about these blind dates. Years later, my son Jared went off to Malone College in Canton, Ohio. One February night he called home and said, "I just met someone on a blind date tonight," and he went on to describe his positive experience. I thought fondly of my blind dating service in college as he talked.

The next year Rachel Luke became his wife.

6

ROMANTIC FAUX PAS

"Romantic" is an umbrella term that covers a lot of territory. It can run all the way from showing affection for a person you're in love with, to feelings of intrigue and attraction for a stranger. Even flirting is a form of romance. The episodes that follow chronicle some of my collegiate romantic missteps.

When I arrived at the Moody Bible Institute in Chicago, Illinois, many were the attractive girls on campus. There was only one problem – I was too shy to ask them out.

One night I slipped up. Some of the guys were hanging out in the dorm when the subject of girls came up. I told them there was someone I thought was cute but admitted that I was too shy to ask her out. The guys took over. They kept insisting, "You can do it! Go ask her out." I steadfastly resisted.

They wouldn't take no for an answer; they hatched a plot on site. Surrounding me, they announced that I was going to ask her out – right then. With that, they picked me up and carried me across campus to Houghton Hall, the women's dorm. No amount of wiggling and pleading helped to release me. I was petrified.

When we arrived at the women's dorm, the usually locked rear entrance door was open. I was carried to the wall phone in the lobby by the elevators. Someone got the girl's number from the lobby desk. They shoved the receiver to my head and dialed her number.

I prayed that she wouldn't answer the phone but, of course, she did. Trembling, with the male audience surrounding me, I identified myself and asked her out. Cheers went up in the lobby as I turned bright shades of red.

The guys each gave me a little money to take her someplace to eat. I'm quite sure this was to make up for what they had put me through. I remember everything well up to the phone call, but I draw a complete blank as to who it was and where we went. Maybe it's romantic trauma.

I never shared my romantic inclinations in the dorm again! And I dated no one else that year.

* * *

The next year, another girl in the women's dorm caught my eye. I was working up courage to ask her out when the women's dorm held an open house. We guys went from floor to floor visiting all the lady students' rooms. I was hoping to see the girl that attracted me. I did! She was in the 4th floor lounge as part of a skit.

There sat four girls from that floor in a line of chairs side by side. In front of them was a little table with a glass of water, toothpaste, and a toothbrush. The first girl brushed her teeth and swished her mouth with the water, spitting it back into the glass when she was finished. She then passed everything to the second girl. She followed suit. The glass of water, toothpaste, and toothbrush went to the third girl and then to the fourth. Each followed suit.

Guess who was sitting in the fourth chair. It was the girl I wanted to ask for a date! She also put the toothpaste on the brush and brushed her teeth. She rinsed her mouth with the murky water in the glass.

And then, she drank the contents of the glass!

All aspirations to ask that girl for a date vanished forever. It was the date that never was. *She* made the faux pas and never knew it. Any romantic feelings had fizzled.

* * *

A southern belle from Tennessee, Ellen Maynard, made her entrance on campus my senior year. She swept me off my feet. By this time, I was well-practiced in dating, so it wasn't a challenge to ask her out.

It was a double-date in Gino's Pizza. We were joking and laughing to hide any nervousness.

She started to tell a joke. It was about a girl and a guy at a dance. The girl had a wooden leg and the guy a wooden eye. Neither were dancing. He walked up to her and said, "Would you like to dance?"

"Would I?!" exclaimed the girl. To which the guy retorted, "Peg leg! Peg leg!"

I had just filled my mouth with Coke when she said, "Would I?" Exploding in laughter, Coke shot across the table completely spritzing her face and blouse. She got past it, but a few more dates and that was it. The romance was short-lived.

* * *

Another girl entered school in the same class as the southern belle. We became friends. I wasn't immediately attracted to her but she was to me, although I didn't know it. One night at dinner in the campus dining room, I went over to the table where she was going to sit. As she sat down, she lifted up slightly from her chair to adjust her skirt.

At precisely the same moment, I arrived at the back of her chair. I was going to help her be seated. As she lifted from her chair seat, I

24

lifted up on the back of her chair. The sudden lack of weight caused the chair to swing back towards me. As she settled back down, there was no chair seat to receive her. She landed smack on her bottom, almost disappearing under the table.

Of course, everyone saw it. And everyone, including the girl, thought it was intentional. It wasn't. It took some serious explaining in the midst of all the laughter. The only bruise she got was to her ego. She finally believed me and accepted my apology.

In the end, this misstep paid off. The girl was Marie Simmons. She eventually became my wife.

7

ROOM INSPECTIONS

Two dorm room inspections in the same week at the end of my freshman year could have played havoc with my return to school the following fall.

Room inspection #1. We had dorm room mothers at the Moody Bible Institute. They'd inspect our rooms for cleanliness with surprise visits. My roommate, Gerald Dafoe, would generally take the lion's share of the cleaning work and we'd always pass inspection.

The end of the Spring semester came, and with it, the dorm mother's final room inspection. Gerald had to leave campus early for the summer, so I told him that I'd prepare our room for the year-end inspection. I never got around to it. Our dorm Mom never showed, and it was time for me to head home for the summer. I locked our dorm room door and took off across campus.

I thought I was in the clear when suddenly I spotted Mom Harl, the dorm mother, coming in my direction. She smiled as she stopped me.

"Hi, Mom. I'm on my way home for the summer," I deflected.

"Oh," she replied, "I was just on my way to inspect your room. You can go, but I only have one question. Is your room well-dusted?"

Decision time. *Do I lie or tell her the truth?* My room, in fact, was "well-dusted" because it was covered with dust.

Her question sparked an immediate response. Before I knew it, out came my "truthful" answer. "Yes, Mom. My room is well-dusted." My response meant one thing to me. It was soon to mean another thing to her. But for the present, I had dodged a bullet.

When I returned in the Fall, Mom Harl and I had an interesting conversation! Then she chuckled as she admitted that my response had been swift and creatively truthful.

Room inspection #2. I'll never forget my encounter with Mr. Landreth, the head custodian, the week before Gerald left school for the summer. Although my meeting with Mr. Landreth took place at the end of the school year, the backstory began in December.

Finals can be stressful, especially in your first semester of college in the snowy, cold, and windy city of Chicago.

College was a different ballgame from high school. I got by academically in high school, but I was an average student with poor study habits. College was a wake-up call and I answered it, but it was hard work.

On this particular Saturday morning, finals were over and I felt a tremendous relief. I delayed my shower, enjoying a lazy morning for the first time in quite a while. With lunch about to be served, however, I knew I'd better get going.

I grabbed a new bar of soap and a towel. It was off to the bathroom across the hall for my shower. I suddenly halted. I wanted just one more moment to unwind from the tension of the past week.

For some reason, I thought about baseball. I was a staunch Phillies baseball fan at the time. I knew the names and stats of all the players. I often dreamed that I could manage the team better than Gene Mauch, the manager. I had no idea that I'd soon transition to being a fanatic

Chicago Cubs fan as a Moody student.

Having stopped in my tracks in my dorm room, I focused on the raised panels that intersected on the room door. I envisioned a strike zone and suddenly I became a Phillies pitcher. I was about to hurl my bar of soap for a perfect strike into the waiting paneled door. My roommate, Gerald, became a silent spectator for this unusual sporting maneuver.

Above the door was an old-fashioned transom window. You don't see them anymore and most young people would have no idea what it is. A transom window sits above the door on bottom hinges with a long, skinny bar that extends down the side of the door trim. When you adjust the handle and bar, the window opens inward to the room to enhance air circulation.

I never gave the transom window a thought.

I took that bar of soap and drew back my right arm. At the same time, I lifted my leg on my imaginary pitcher's mound and uttered, "The windup and the pitch!" With that, I released the "ball."

It was a wild pitch. The bar of soap slipped out of my hand and soared upward at a high rate of speed. In a split second, the "ball" crashed through the transom window, exploding glass shards in every direction. Gerald's jaw dropped in disbelief. He didn't have to say it; I knew what he was thinking: *I don't think that was the smartest thing you've ever done.*

I was in shock. I knew the damage should be reported, but I had no extra money. I was a poor freshman in a big city. Then I remembered the building was scheduled for demolition the following year. Justifying it to myself, I decided to keep quiet about it and hope for the best. I knew Gerald wouldn't turn me in.

The end of the spring semester arrived, and it was time to go home for summer break. The window stayed broken all that time. *Since the building was doomed anyway, no real harm done,* I continued to tell myself. Soon I'd be home free.

Unscheduled room inspections happened the last week of the school year. Sure enough, someone knocked on our dorm room door. It was Mr. Landreth, head of the custodial department. My antenna went up as he said, "We're doing our year-end inspection, and I notice that your transom window is broken. What happened?"

I had to think quickly. I decided to tell him the truth but not the whole story.

"Well, someone was in my room a while back. He was messing around and accidentally broke the window. It was the last thing he intended to do."

"Okay," said Mr. Landreth. "Can you give me his name and dorm room number?" I had to think quickly, *Okay, I'll give him my name and room number and he'll have the information he needs, but he won't know it's me.*

I replied, "Sure. His name is Al Detter, and his room number is 214." Mr. Landreth thanked me and gently closed the door as he walked away.

I breathed a sigh of relief and congratulated myself that I could tell the truth and yet dodge a bullet. Gerald had a wry grin on his face and an expression like, *It's not going to be that easy.*

Just then there was another knock on our door. It was the last person I expected to see. Mr. Landreth was back! He said, "This is Room 214!"

Sheepishly I replied, "Yes, and I'm Al Detter." I was exposed and embarrassed. His eyes twinkled and he smiled as if to say, *Boys will be boys.* Soon he was gone.

I never got a bill. The building came down.

And for my remaining years as a student and for many years after, every time I saw Mr. Landreth, he'd smile as if to say, *Your secret is safe with me.*

8

THE SURPRISE

Six days on. Two days off. That was my schedule. I was a Chicago Transit Authority bus driver during the summers while I was in college. I loved my job.

In many jobs, it's five days of work with two days off. But I adjusted to the six-days on, two days off schedule. No day was alike so the week would fly by.

There was a sense of accomplishment in driving the bus. I come from a small rural town where school buses were common. But city buses? They were never part of my growing up experience.

The first time I got on a bus in Chicago as a student, I thought to myself, *There's no way in the world I'd ever want to be a city bus driver. It's multi-tasking on steroids.* You had to concentrate on traffic, especially in rush hour. There were mirrors and clearances and crazy drivers and turn signals. You had to change the route numbers and destinations on the front of the bus. Front and rear doors had to be opened and closed at just the right time.

During rush hour, crowds would mob the bus with their money and transfers. You had to make change quickly and punch the transfers correctly. Timing was everything because you had to be on schedule.

Supervisors in unmarked cars were stationed along the route to ensure you did a good job. I thought, *Driving a huge rig isn't for me. I'll never do that job!*

But money talked. I was a poor college student, and it was the best paying summer job in town. Next thing I knew, I was down at the bus employment office applying for a job. I was hired. Soon the job I feared became second nature. I couldn't believe how good a driver this small-town guy had become in Chicago.

I was also engaged to be marreid. During the summer, my fiancée, Marie Simmons, lived 180 miles south in Peoria, Illinois. Marie and I got together when we could, but our schedules kept us apart more than we wanted.

On the sixth day of one of my weeks, I created this compelling plan, *When I get off at midnight, I'm going to drive to Peoria to surprise Marie.* I didn't tell anyone, not even her father. I figured that I could sleep on their sofa or even in my car if necessary. I drove my bus route with great anticipation. I could hardly wait.

Midnight finally came and I jumped into my 1967 Volkswagen Bug. The car seemed to know its way there. *Marie is going to be one shocked lady when I appear! She's going to love it,* I mused. I could just envision the surprise!

I rolled up to her house around 2:30am. The dwelling was understandably dark. I was sure that awakening the house with my unexpected presence would be a forgivable offense. In her excitement, I knew Marie would have my back with her father.

I knocked on the door. Soon a lone light appeared from the living room. The door slowly opened. It was my future father-in-law. There was a look of stunned surprise on his face and then a broad, bemused grin.

I spoke first. "I got off work tonight and decided to drive down to surprise Marie. Can you get her?" I asked with great anticipation.

"Well, sure," came the reply. "But there's only one problem. Marie left earlier tonight to drive to Chicago to surprise *you!*"

I was in disbelief! Surely, he had to be jesting. But he wasn't. "Please, can I use your phone?" I implored. (This was long before cellphones.) I knew there had to be an outside chance that he was kidding. Like doubting Thomas, I needed to hear her voice to be sure.

I called my apartment in Chicago. One of my roommates answered the phone and soon I heard her voice. "Where *are* you?" I said with anticipation and animation. She replied, "I'm in Chicago. I came up to surprise you. Where are *you?!*"

When Marie got to Chicago late that evening and learned from my roommates that I had gone to Peoria, she too was in total disbelief. She assured me that they were being great hosts. But neither of us could believe what had happened.

I never set foot in the house. I told her father, "See you later; it's off to Chicago!" And down the road I went. All the way back, I tried to figure the odds of what had just transpired. Maybe it was a million to one. I arrived at 5:00am and Marie and I were finally together. That was all that mattered.

Instead of ships, it was two cars passing in the night – a night we'll always remember with sheer amazement and laughter.

9

THE KICK

Sometimes teasing backfires.

I'm not sure if teasing is part of a person's DNA but, from my earliest memories, I was a tease. The extreme form of teasing for me was practical jokes.

My family, immediate and extended, knew this about me, and it was an accepted fact. For the most part, it was enjoyed. I seemed to have a knack for knowing where to draw the line. My teasing rarely turned into long-term annoyance.

The teasing side of me was part of my familiarity with others in this respect: if I knew someone well, part of my affection was expressed through teasing. I felt free to have some fun with the people closest to me. I guess you could describe it as one of my love languages.

But if I didn't know someone well, teasing was rare. Especially at church. But when I went on trips with church people, the teasing would bleed through. I've taken fourteen trips to Israel, one trip to Haiti, one trip to the Philippines, and one trip to West Africa with various groups. My traveling companions would all exclaim, "We never saw this side of you at church!" They liked it.

The big teasing assumption early in my marriage was, *I'm sure Marie will like it, too.* I never gave much thought to the contrary because it was just part of my family culture growing up. Even though Marie wasn't used to teasing in her family of origin, I thought, *Teasing will be a blessing for her!*

We got married and, yes, part of the package was my teasing.

It wasn't long until she adapted to my style and dished it back. That wasn't something I was ready for. She also learned how to get the upper hand.

And so it was in our first year of marriage that we found ourselves enjoying the ambiance of Buckingham Fountain in Chicago. It was a newlyweds date. We held hands and walked around the fountain, enjoying the occasional spray. Then the time came for us to leave.

Being newlyweds, we were short on money but rich in love. We had "splurged" just a little on a basic 1967 Volkswagen Bug: tan, stick shift, no air conditioning, roll-up windows, chrome bumpers, and a small trunk in the front. But I viewed the car like a prized Cadillac. There are times I still wish I had that car.

As we left the fountain, I got into the car first and a teasing urge overcame me. I locked her door. She tried to get in, but I wouldn't open it. She knocked on the door. I chuckled. She persisted. Then she came around to my door. It was locked.

She went back to her door again – a little more pleading, a little more knocking, a Cheshire grin on my face, a grimace on hers. Suddenly, she drew back her leg and gave her door a kick, a hard kick. It shook the car. All I could envision was a half caved-in passenger door.

Instinctively, I leaped from the car and ran around to the passenger door to survey the damage. Cars were built well in those days. Remarkably, there wasn't a mark on the door.

But I suddenly became aware of something.

As I ran to check out the damage, Marie dashed to the driver's side of the car and climbed in. You guessed it. She locked the door. I was stunned. She gave the kick and I took the bait. And now it was *me* on the sidewalk begging for her to open the door.

Finally, she relented. It was from that day forward that I realized she didn't always think my teasing was funny. The kick on the door was her signal to me. But it was also a signal that I had a pretty smart wife, so I'd better watch my step!

10

THE STOVE

No matter how well you plan, some things just plain go wrong. While in Dallas, Marie and I managed 16 apartments during our last three years in seminary. They were studio apartments arranged in a U-shaped building with a courtyard in the middle. I used to think it would be a perfect set for a movie musical. On cue, all the front doors would open as people came out singing and dancing in a beautifully choreographed scene in the courtyard.

But overseeing the Grandview Apartments wasn't that easy.

Seminary was busy enough and the duties of managing apartments took up most of our free time. Our duties included filling vacancies, refreshing and painting empty apartments for the next tenants, cutting the grass, trimming the hedges, and miscellaneous maintenance.

And of course, there were problems to solve like: complaints about noisy neighbors, leaky faucets, clogged toilets, strange odors, invisible bugs, and malfunctioning appliances.

Managing apartments had its risks. One tenant didn't like my impromptu inspection. That night he kicked a dent in my car door. Another time, the hedges needed trimming, which brought me to a most unfortunate trifecta: I hit a bee's nest and got stung; I stepped on a snake, making a shriek that could be heard throughout Dallas; and since I'm colorblind, I never saw the orange cord in the hedge of green leaves. Soon there was a loud pop and flash as I severed the cord with the clippers.

And then there were neighborly relations that had to be maintained.

We had a studio piano in our apartment and Marie liked to practice almost every day. One day she was rehearsing a classical piece and she played it over and over again.

Knock, knock, knock on our back door. It was the next door neighbor. We shared a common wall. "For heaven's sake! Will you stop playing that song?" he implored. We were as nice as pie and assured him that he would never hear that song again. Marie struck it from her repertoire.

We were childless at the time and so were some friends who came to visit us, Vern and Connie Gahman. They were good friends from my Souderton, Pennsylvania, high school days and on a 9-week sightseeing trip around the country. We were to spend three days together, having fun, and catching up on each other's lives.

A day or two before our friends arrived, the guy who complained about Marie's music saw me in the courtyard and said, "There's something wrong with our stove. Could you check it out and fix it?" He told me what the problem was, and I assured him that I'd take care of it.

I turned every knob and dial on the stove. I checked the interior. Everything worked perfectly, but he insisted that the problem still lingered. Sometimes in customer service, you placate even when all is well. I had a few extra stoves in my utility shed, so I assured him that I'd swap his for a newer model. He was happy.

On day two of our friends' sojourn with us, I said to Vern, "How'd you like to help me swap out a stove in the apartment next to us." He agreed, and off we went to the shed. I found the stove I wanted and loaded it on the dolly. With all confidence I said, "The stove's not that heavy and we don't have that far to go. We don't need to use the strap."

When we got to the back door of the apartment, we unloaded the newer stove just to the left of the three concrete steps going up to the door. The next move was to bring the old stove down those steps and out to the shed. The newer stove would then take its place in the kitchen.

We loaded the old stove onto the dolly. Once again I said to Vern, "It's only three steps down. We don't need to strap it on. I'll take the front and you take the rear."

Propping open the door, we began the descent. Step one – a little wobble. Step two – a major wobble with the shifting of weight. Step three – an uncontrollable lunge to the left, with the stove exiting the dolly.

It was one of those events when time moves in slow motion. You see it happening and you can't do a thing about it. You watch in absolute disbelief.

The next thing we knew, there was a loud crash of metal hitting metal as the old stove hit the newer stove and landed on its side. There were dents galore, with burner parts and porcelain exploding everywhere.

That was not a very sanctified moment for me. I blurted out the unexpected as Vern's and my eyes met and locked in anguished disbelief, "Holy s—!"

Marie and Connie happened to arrive just before the crash and witnessed the whole debacle.

When I'm in trouble, Marie emphatically calls out my full first and middle names. When she said, "Alfred Lee!" I knew I was in trouble. It wasn't about the damage to the stoves. It was about what I had uttered after the crash.

Both stoves were damaged beyond repair. Thankfully, I had another stove in the shed. This time, we used the strap on the dolly to transport it. Fortunately, my boss Joe Foster was an understanding man. In similar fashion, Marie finally afforded me an umbrella of mercy.

The visit of our friends was forever branded by the crashing of the stoves. Whenever we get together, we relive that moment. And laugh. And my expletive? It lives in infamy.

11

THE SERMON

A friend commented to me about my most recent sermon online and he paid me a compliment. At least he didn't say what one dear saint told his pastor, "Each sermon you preach is better than the next one."

It's nearly a miracle that I can remember *any* sermon I preached just several weeks before, let alone sermons and speeches from nearly fifty years ago. But I clearly remember one of them. It was back in seminary in homiletics class.

Homiletics can be defined as "the application of general principles of rhetoric to the specific art of public preaching." In the class, we began by learning how to give persuasive speeches. After persuasive speeches, we were taught the basics of sermonizing. We learned how to fashion an introduction and conclusion around the body of the sermon, ignited by "the big idea."

The flow of the sermon was important, so we were taught "unity, order, and progress." We were coached on how to make the sermon memorable via a number of literary devices. And of course, delivery. You mess that up and you sink the sermon no matter how good the content may be.

This idea of making the sermon "memorable" intrigued me. But I had no clue that what I said in my sermon that day would be remembered for years to come.

My text was Philippians 3:8-11, where the Apostle Paul says: *Indeed, I count everything as loss because of the surpassing worth of knowing Christ Jesus my Lord. For His sake I have suffered the loss of all things and count them as rubbish, in order that I may gain Christ and be found in Him, not having a righteousness of my own that comes from the law, but that which comes through faith in Christ, the righteousness from God that depends on faith, that I may know Him and the power of His resurrection, and may share His sufferings, becoming like Him in His death, that by any means possible I may attain the resurrection from the dead.*

That's such a classic passage (and run-on sentence). I wanted to make it come alive by first setting it up with compelling background information. Philippians is a book about joy. Yet Paul was in a cruel Roman prison when he wrote it. Paul's loss of everything under difficult conditions, while in prison, would surely drive home the point.

I continued by painting a picture of Paul's prison circumstances as I set up the text. And then came the memorable line that has lived in infamy until this day. Referring to the prison I said, "Paul had it all: pedigree, posterity, power, prestige, position. But because of the surpassing worth of knowing Christ, he gave it all up. All of it! There sat Paul, shackled in chains – in that dark, dank, dingy, dirty, derelict dungeon!"

There it was, a classic literary device called alliteration – a way to highlight a short phrase with each word beginning with the same sound – delivered perfectly for effect. I said it with passion, hoping to arouse some empathetic emotions from my classmate audience.

But it didn't happen. No empathy. No compassion. No amazement. Instead, the class burst into laughter. My mnemonic device had utterly failed.

Undaunted, I continued my sermon in recovery mode and finished to applause. Professor Reed commented on the strengths and weaknesses of my sermon. And he just couldn't let it go about that "dark, dank, dingy, dirty, derelict dungeon."

And neither can the classmates that I stay in touch with. Invariably they recall that day decades ago. We laugh and relive the moment.

I learned my lesson. It was a perfect example of "too much of a good thing." I put excessive alliteration in mothballs from that day forward.

But what about other aspects of sermon delivery?

When my son Jared was small, his mom asked him if he'd ever like to be a preacher like his dad. "No," he said, "I don't want to yell at people."

Good grief! Preaching is complicated.

12

THE KISS

A s previously mentioned, Marie and I managed a small apartment complex in Dallas, Texas during my seminary years. The tenants ranged in age from graduate students to the very elderly. Sometimes the job was a pain. More often, it was a steady source of human interest.

Colorful characters lived in some of the apartments. Requests were common: *Shampoo my rug, exterminate my apartment for bugs* (which didn't exist), *fix my leaky faucet, get me new carpeting, provide me with a new lock set.* But Marguerite Drake, one of the elderly tenants, made the most frequent and unusual request of all.

We tried to build a good relationship with each of our tenants, and we did the best we could to accommodate their requests. Each month, I went the extra mile. I'd go to their apartments to collect the rent; they didn't have to come to me.

I'd knock on the door. I'd greet them when they'd answer, and we'd exchange a few pleasantries. I'd ask them how things were going and what we could do for them. They'd place the check in my hand.

It was different with Marguerite. At the end of each monthly conversation, she'd say, "I have a favor to ask. Won't you give an old lady a kiss?"

The first time I was taken aback. I thought I had misunderstood her. I said goodbye and away I went.

The next month, the same thing happened: "Won't you give an old lady a kiss?"

I chuckled and said, "Sorry, Marguerite. I only kiss my wife."

She wouldn't be deterred. Each month at the end of my collection visit, she'd pose the same question, "Won't you give an old lady a kiss?"

Marguerite reminded me of the widow in Luke 18. She kept coming to the judge to ask for legal protection from her opponent. He finally relented and issued a protection order, saying, "Lest, she will wear me out." I had long determined that Marguerite would never wear me out.

It was nearly a year with this kind of badgering when Marguerite changed her strategy. As we got to the moment for her request, she said, "Today is my 75th birthday. Won't you give an old lady a kiss? It would make me so happy."

I entered into an internal debate: From *Forget it and get out of there* to *What could be so bad about giving an old lady a peck on the cheek on her birthday?* I settled on the latter.

"Okay, Marguerite. A peck on your cheek for your birthday, just this one time."

Her eyes brightened, and a grin spanned her wrinkled face. I couldn't wait until my Good Samaritan act was accomplished. In slow motion, she turned her face to the right to provide my lips a landing place on her cheek. I leaned forward to kiss her.

In an instant, Marguerite turned her head. Now face to face, she lunged toward me and planted a sloppy wet kiss right on my lips. I was stunned and grossed out all in one sudden emotion.

"See you later, Marguerite!" I exclaimed and bolted like a scared rabbit. I ran across the apartment courtyard and bounded like a speeding bullet up the stairs of our studio apartment. Marie saw the blur passing by and followed me up the stairs to our bathroom.

I repeatedly spit into the sink, dousing my mouth with mouthwash and vociferously brushing my teeth.

"What's wrong with you?" queried my confused wife. "What just happened?"

"Marguerite kissed me on the lips!" I managed. Once the oral remedies were completed, I told Marie the story. She already knew about the monthly requests.

Marie's radar would turn on if she ever thought some woman was coming on to me. But Marguerite? She was like a toothless lioness. Instead of any rush of caution or anger, Marie couldn't stop laughing. It took me a while, but soon I was laughing with her.

Upon reflection, it wasn't just the kiss itself that stunned me. It was the unsettling lip to lip wetness. And the fact that Marguerite had found a way to outwit me royally!

Starting the next month and ever thereafter, Marie collected Marguerite's rent.

13

CAR TALK

As newlyweds, Marie and I lived on a meager $30 a week and depended on public transportation in Chicago. It soon became evident that we needed our own set of wheels. A great bargain price of $195 was struck for a 1962 Corvair, arguably one of the most flawed cars ever made. But I was convinced that *our* Corvair would be different.

It wasn't. It wouldn't start in the rain. It wouldn't start in the cold. It wouldn't start for any number of reasons. We were stranded countless times, and frustrations were mounting.

On a subzero night in Chicago, that unreliable bucket of bolts once again wouldn't start. *That* was the night I first fell from grace with my newlywed wife. I determined that the gas line was frozen and informed Marie of my diagnosis as she sat shivering in the front passenger seat of the lifeless car. Across the street was a convenience store. With no money to spare, I grudgingly bought a can of *HEET*, a gasoline antifreeze.

My fingers froze as I unscrewed the bottle cap, opened the little fender gas tank door, and removed the gas tank cap. Turning the bottle upside down, I aimed it at the tank opening. Suddenly, I felt liquid all over my feet. The gas tank pipe in that model car was separated from the fender by about an inch. The entire contents baptized my feet.

My carnality got the upper hand and I exclaimed, "I'll be d*mned!" I thought I had whispered it. But when I got in the car, my shocked wife inquired, "Did I just hear what I think I heard?"

Marie was quick to forgive her new husband. And we had one of the best laughs of our early marriage when I picked up the paper several days later and saw a cartoon with the following caption, *I'll never buy another used car. I don't have the vocabulary to run it.*

We unloaded that Corvair and got a great deal on a 1967 VW Bug, with no air-conditioning. Like the Corvair, it had a rear-engine, but this one behaved itself, at least in the beginning. We ran it all over Chicago and down to seminary in Dallas, Texas. I piled on the miles.

With no money to spare as students, when we saw an advertisement for three free days at a resort eighty miles south of Dallas, we jumped on it. All we had to do was listen to a presentation. With eager anticipation, we got on the freeway for our much-needed respite. Halfway there, the car began to sputter and make scary engine noises. It came to an abrupt stop just as I pulled onto the berm – a blown engine.

To this day, I don't know how we got the car back to Dallas and still arrive at the resort on time. But this I know. I had been amazed at how cheaply I could run that car. The reason? I ran it nearly 95,000 miles without changing the oil and filters. I never thought of it.

I learned a huge lesson about "saving" money and maintenance.

We got $500 for the Bug and bought a brand-new 1974 Toyota Corona. In those days, many cars didn't come with air-conditioning. You need AC in Dallas. So when I bought the car, I emphasized that I wanted *factory air.* I thought an after-market air conditioner would be less reliable. The salesman threw it in as part of the deal. I was so proud of my bargaining abilities.

We finally had an air-conditioned car.

That summer we drove to California in our brand-new car. We were elated with the cold air. On the return trip, we were remarking how wonderful it was to have air-conditioning. We had every assurance that we'd return to Dallas in comfort.

Wrong! On Interstate 10, in the 100-plus degree desert heat of Arizona, the air-conditioning went kaput. The vent air came at us like a furnace. There was nothing we could do to coax the cold air to return. A service station attendant told us he couldn't help us, and that we had a problematic aftermarket air-conditioning unit.

Aftermarket?! I had ordered factory air!

We rolled down our windows and endured the hottest and sweatiest ride of our lives.

I knew where I was going once back in Dallas – straight to the Toyota dealer. Fuming, I found the salesperson and laid into him as far as a seminary student could without crossing the sin line. I squawked, "I asked for factory air, not an aftermarket unit!"

He gently led me to my car. We got inside and he showed me the emblem on the AC knob. It read *Factory Aire*. It was an aftermarket product with the brand name *Factory Aire*.

"A mild form of deception," I protested, waving the surrender flag. They fixed it for free.

These days, I still look for car bargains. I'm a little smarter about sales tricks. And I've learned the all-important lesson of maintenance along the way!

14

THE SHOTS

Shots have always been scary for me.

In grade school, we had to be inoculated for measles, mumps, and chicken pox. It was also at the tail-end of the polio era, and we had to get a circular pattern of serum pinpricks in our upper left arm. I didn't cry, but there was an element of trauma.

During my growing up years, other shots were part of my life – Novocain at the dentist, tetanus at the doctor, needles and IVs for a tonsillectomy, that sort of thing. Mind you, it wasn't like I was the only one on the end of a sharp needle. Shots are everyone's plight. But I've always been especially averse to them, to put it mildly.

When it came time for me to get married, we made the mandatory trip to the courthouse. In those days, blood tests were required so couples would know if there were potential difficulties, like the RH Factor. The technician inserted the needle to draw blood and I passed out.

As I've gotten older, I've learned to tolerate needles. When it's time for blood to be drawn or an IV started, I tense up, close my eyes, and turn my head away from the action. Marie thinks it's kind of amusing, and I give her that.

When Marie and I were dating, we talked about having children.

Agreeing that we wanted four, we thought it would happen as a matter of course. It didn't. Seven and a half years went by before we had our first child, Jason, by adoption.

Adoption happened only after we exhausted every avenue of achieving a pregnancy known to us at that time. There was a continual cycle of hope and disappointment. As we tried, it was medical procedure after medical procedure for both Marie and me. And you guessed it – needles were part of the process. Marie did great. Me? Not so well.

One day Dr. Dennis said, "I'm not sure what the exact problem is. I think both of you have contributing issues. But I think Al is the bigger reason. Let's try one last option." We listened intently.

"We're going to give Al a hormone. He'll need thirty shots and you, his dear wife, will administer them." She smiled while I turned white. Thirty shots were equivalent to walking the plank as far as I was concerned.

"Surely you jest," I protested.

"No, not at all," he replied. "You're going to get thirty shots. I give you a better than even chance for achieving a pregnancy on this regimen."

I swallowed hard and said meekly, "Okay."

I expected to walk out of the office and come back later for another visit in order to start the procedure.

That's when he said, "I'm going to write you a prescription. You'll get thirty needles and enough serum for thirty shots. You'll need to refrigerate the serum." He continued, "Marie, I'm going to show you how to give Al his shots." I expected a verbal and visual demonstration, like sticking a needle in an orange.

What he said next weakened my knees. "Al, please drop your pants and underpants and lean over the table like you're getting a prostate exam." I knew he was serious, and my blood ran cold.

In that position, I couldn't see what they were doing; I could only hear. This nightmare couldn't be over fast enough.

The doctor said to Marie, "You take the needle like this. And don't be timid. Think of it as a dart and kind of throw it into his rump."

He let it fly. Thud! I broke into a profuse sweat.

Then he said, "You're in fatty tissue. If you don't like the position of the needle or if you draw blood, all you need to do is to withdraw it a little and move it to its desired position." And with that, he moved the needle in and out and around four or five times. I was on the verge of trauma. It was just another day's work for him.

Marie was fine with it, but she knew what was happening in my mind as she showed some compassion by a tender tap on my bare hip.

"Do you think you can do it?" he asked. Marie said, "I'm fine. The question is, can Al do it?" I pulled up my pants and exited as quickly as possible. The Tribulation was about to begin.

The next day was the launch – shot #1. I dropped my drawers and leaned over the dining room table. My hands grew cold and I closed my eyes. I felt the cotton ball with alcohol cleanse the target. It seemed like an eternity as Marie hesitated with the needle. Both of us were nervous. She let the needle go and it was true to its mark. I took the hit and remained standing.

We'd repeat that process every three days until 30 shots were accomplished. It was amazing. With each shot there was less anxiety. By the time thirty shots were finished, it was routine. I suppose you can get accustomed to anything.

Several months later, Marie whispered in my ear, "I think I'm pregnant!" She was! In October, we welcomed Jared, our second child, into our home.

That was many years ago. But over the years, even to this day, we recall the needle ritual. In bed, Marie will rub my bum like she has a cotton ball in her hand. There'll be a brief pause. And then her index finger will touch me like she's administering a shot. It's a tender reminder that what I greatly feared produced what we deeply desired. And we both smile with satisfaction and delight.

15

LITTLE BUGS

I n our early years of marriage, when money was scarce, we had to make do. We weren't starving, but neither did we have an abundance of food in the kitchen.

It had been a long day at the church. Marie had prepared a tasty dinner but, just before bedtime, I was feeling a little hungry.

We lived in the Central Time Zone in Northbrook, Illinois. In that time zone, the news came on at 10:00pm. Our evening ritual was to watch the news till 10:30pm, prepare to retire, and then climb into bed to Nightsounds with Bill Pearce on WMBI radio. The clock timer shut it off around 11:00pm.

My hunger led me to the kitchen just before the news. The living room was dimly lit from the light of the TV. The light of an electric candle in the kitchen window seemed sufficient for my mission.

I checked out the refrigerator. Nothing much there but there was some milk. I felt around in the pantry. Nothing much there either. Back to the refrigerator. Back to the pantry. You know the drill. I dug a little deeper. Behind a box on a shelf, I felt the shape of a cereal box that had been long forgotten. In my mind I exclaimed, *Food! Bedtime snack! I'm in luck!*

My instincts said, *Turn on the light as you prepare your feast.* I disregarded that idea and opened the cupboard door. A cereal dish was very discernible in the dim light. It was just as easy to capture a spoon from the silverware drawer. And an open refrigerator door? Just enough light to pour the milk on the cereal.

I arrived in the living room to the familiar sound of the opening music for the news. I congratulated myself for not missing anything and took a seat on the sofa, the TV to my left. I sat somewhat closer to the TV than normal because I wanted it to shed a little more light on my cereal bowl. I thought about turning on the lamp that was sitting on the end table next to the sofa armrest, but once again decided against it.

Some faint kind of warning intuition was working within me from the start of this whole escapade. I couldn't identify it and it wasn't strong enough, so I disregarded it.

Spoonful number one went down the hatch. Spoonful number two. Something was a little odd. Spoonful number three. *I think I'll turn on the light,* I finally decided.

There I saw a shadowy convention of little creatures in my cereal. I screamed in horror. Marie was sitting across the room. She went on high alert. I bolted to her side and handed her the bowl. Looking away, I queried her with high tension, "Do you see anything that doesn't belong in that bowl?" I retreated to the other side of the room with my index fingers ready to stop up my ears.

She replied calmly but firmly, "Yes, the cereal is loaded with weevil larvae." Incredulous, I shrieked, "No! No! You're kidding me! Don't tell me! Don't tell me!"

"Sorry to say," she replied, "It's full of weevils."

"No! No!" I shouted again, as if my protests would change reality, "Tell me it isn't true! Tell me it isn't true!"

"Al," she said, "come over here and look."

"No! No! Tell me it isn't true!" I said once more, as my stomach began to quake.

I ran toward the bathroom to a series of dry heaves. Rarely had my mouth ever experienced as much brushing and mouthwash as it did that night.

I returned to the living room. The offending bowl was still in Marie's hands. I didn't get near her as she suggested that I take a look and then dispose of it. I had expected more sympathy by this time.

"No! I can't look at it," I retorted. "You're going to have to dispose of it."

She did, along with the tainted box of cereal. My body shook involuntarily every time I thought about what had happened.

The larvae had not yet hatched into bugs. And, to this day, I'm not sure which would have been the lesser of "two weevils."

But I can assure you, from that night on, I have judiciously inspected every cereal box from which I have ever eaten.

16

THE CHILDREN'S STORY

Sometimes it's not the names or words that are spoken – or mangled, but *how* they're spoken, that creates a humorous situation. Sometimes it's as simple as inflection, which the following story illustrates.

As Senior Pastor of a church, rare were the Sundays when I could visit another church. That mainly happened when I was on vacation.

Some years back, my Aunt Millie and Uncle John were part of a startup church in Pottstown, Pennsylvania. A previous church there had fallen on hard times and closed. A few people in the area had a vision to start a new church in the old building. A core group launched Sunday morning worship services there.

Startup churches don't usually have large numbers to work with. They don't have many staff members or multiple programs. They get by with a small cadre of volunteers to do the essentials, hoping that they'll catch a wave of momentum and grow.

When they knew we were coming for a visit, Uncle John and Aunt Millie invited us to come with them to their church. We were happy to oblige. There were about 50 people gathered in the sanctuary. They had a nursery but no other programs for children. That meant the children from toddlers on up sat with their parents during the worship service.

People arrived early, some for fellowship and some to tend to behind-the-scenes matters that make a service run well. When 9:30am came, everyone settled into their seats. The service moved along in a very predictable way – welcome, announcements, congregational singing, special music, the offering, the sermon, a closing song, and a benediction.

But since the children were in the service, they offered another feature – a children's sermon.

The children were called forward to sit on the floor in front of the person telling the story. Of course, adults love stories as well, so in a small church it was a win-win situation.

The storyteller was introduced. My aunt leaned over and whispered to me, "She's new to our church. In fact, she's new to the faith. She came out of a rough background." The whispering stopped, and I tuned in to the storyteller. It was great to see a brand-new convert becoming active so quickly in the church.

The story explained that *anyone* can serve the Lord. You don't have to be famous. You don't have to be rich. You don't have to be a college graduate. You can just be yourself. Even though you don't think you have much to offer. Even though you might be nervous and new to the faith. *Anyone* can serve Jesus.

The story continued about someone who was invited by a friend to do a church ministry he thought she'd be good at. But the lady objected, "I could never do that."

"Sure," replied the friend, "You'd do a wonderful job."

"Well, so many other people could do it better," she continued. "And other people might think I'm not doing it very well." It was like God calling Moses and Moses raising all kinds of objections.

The dialogue continued back and forth, "I can't do it."

"Yes, you can."

"I might embarrass you."

"No, you won't."

Finally, the friend in the story was out of options. As the storyteller started to make the main point, she read it this way, "You don't have to do it for others or be afraid or even experienced. Just trust in the Lord and *do* it, *for Christ's sake!*"

The reader put heavy emphasis on the "for Christ's sake" part, adding a little frustration in her voice as she said it. She spoke it like a mild form of profanity, instead of an encouragement to do it for the Lord's sake.

At that moment, I was struck with an overwhelming impulse to laugh, which had to be suppressed, lest I ruin the ministry of the storyteller and disrupt the church service. I looked at Marie, and my aunt and uncle looked at me. *That* made things worse. We needed a relief valve for our laughter but there was none. All we could do was stuff it until after the service, fighting back the internal ripples of laughter all the way.

It all made sense: a new convert with an unchurched background, reading a story, as only she knew how to say it. She didn't know the difference.

The lady continued to attend and serve the Lord in the church. No one ever told her about the line that tickled our funny bones. But those of us who were present that morning will never forget that sometimes inflection makes all the difference – especially in church!

17

GROSSED OUT

My friend, Jerry Marshall, has a very weak stomach. When things happen that "gross him out," he has a major reaction. He's just wired that way.

Being his good friend, I should never test him in these matters. I should protect him. I should look out for him. I should spare him any needless moments of anxiety. But honestly, it's kind of fun to observe his reactions. They almost beg me to induce some kind of benign trauma into his life.

There are times I'm totally innocent. Like the time we were at a seafood restaurant. Jerry ordered the seafood sampler. When his meal came, there was a variety of items on his plate, and he wasn't exactly sure what was what.

I called the waiter over on his behalf. "My friend here isn't quite sure what all the items are on his plate. Could you please identify them?" "No problem," came the response. None of us were ready for what we were about to behold.

The waiter proceeded to identify each item on Jerry's plate. But he went one incredible step further. With each piece he identified, he took his index finger and nudged it, pushing each of them around his plate.

Jerry looked at me. His wife Jan looked at him. Marie and I looked at Jerry and then at the waiter with a loss for words. The waiter left.

Jerry swallowed hard. "What are you going to do?" I inquired.

Jerry is a mild-mannered, no complainer kind of guy. Not so much his wife, and not so much Marie or me. But we were all so stunned, we lost our sense of confrontation. We watched Jerry reluctantly eat his previously desired meal.

* * *

But there are times I'm not so innocent. Like the time the four of us were enjoying ourselves at a mall near Lake Chautauqua, New York. We were doing some casual shopping when Jerry and I spied an ice cream shop. We convinced our wives to join us.

Jerry loves milkshakes, and we each ordered one. Jerry made short work of his and drank it down to a remaining tiny remnant. He then excused himself to use the restroom. I was overcome with a tricky idea.

Marie reluctantly gave me one of her long hairs. I carefully placed it so it stuck down the inside of his glass in plain sight. The girls complained mildly but allowed me to complete my antics.

Soon Jerry returned. He picked up his milkshake and brought the glass and straw towards his mouth for the last little bit. It worked perfectly. Jerry saw the hair and let out this little revolting screech. "I can't believe it!" he lamented. "There's a hair in my glass and I drank nearly the whole shake!" His face turned ashen white under his red head of hair.

I felt guilty, and it pushed me to a confession. "Jerry, you *didn't* drink a whole shake with a hair in it. While you were in the men's room, I put the hair on the side of your glass." He was reluctant at first to believe me. But the girls verified my story, and color returned to his face. He looked relieved, and gave me his patented *You are forgiven* look.

* * *

Jerry and I used to play racquetball at our local racquetball club. We were "C" league players. We played a hard but lousy game, but we made a contest out of it. Our pattern was the best of three, the whirlpool, and then off to work.

Jerry loved the whirlpool. It was always a highlight for him following the workout. We'd sit and chat and feel the bubbling current massage our resting bodies.

One day we were relishing the whirlpool when Jerry said how much he enjoyed it. Impulsively I replied, "So do I." Adding a line to tease him, I continued, "It's just too bad that the guys pee in it from time to time."

Do you remember the face color change? It happened again. Jerry stood up and ejected himself from the pool faster than a hunted jack rabbit. "Jerry!" I protested. "I'm kidding! I'm kidding!"

Jerry would have none of it. There was nothing I could say or do to talk him back into the pool. He was gone for good. And I mean, for good. Jerry and I continued to play our best of three racquetball games. But he never set foot in that whirlpool again, or any *other* one for that matter.

Jerry believed that I was kidding him. But reason got the best of him. The odds were high that I was right. And he would never again take that chance.

18

BUCK LURE

When I was young, hunting never appealed to me. Maybe I could understand watching a football game in the cold and snow. But hunting in the rain, wind, cold, snow, or fog? It was not for me.

In 1978, we moved to Erie, Pennsylvania, where I became the Senior Pastor of Grace Baptist Church. And what did I discover but a bunch of hunters in the church.

These men weren't timid. They made it clear they wanted me in the woods with them. The first year I declined, but under pressure. The next year they increased their zeal. I declined again. But just barely.

They wouldn't take "no" for an answer in year three, so I made them a deal.

"If I go with you, you gotta promise that you'll never ask me again. It's a one-time deal and then I'm out for good." We shook hands.

Now came the dilemma of hunting apparel. I had absolutely nothing that would remotely work for hunting. I figured, *When they find this out, they'll let me off the hook.* Not a chance.

The guys drove their 70 miles to hunting camp after their family Thanksgiving festivities. I stayed behind with ministerial duties and finished the Sunday night service. In the darkness of unfamiliar country roads, I made my way to camp. The next day was opening day of buck season.

The group greeted me warmly and, after some snacks, it was off to bed in a somewhat unkempt bachelor's pad. A sound woke me in the middle of the night, a sound I prayed wouldn't happen – the pitter-patter of rain on the roof. I knew serious hunters wouldn't be deterred and, in a couple hours, I'd be dragged into a soupy mess.

Before daylight, we crossed a cow pasture in the drizzle and entered the woods. They soon stationed me at a huge rock. It was "Ray's Rock," they said with affection. One of my hunting companions had a son named Ray.

"You're sure to get a buck from this rock, and Ray's willing to give up his spot. We'll be back to check up on you," said Jack Switzer, his father, as they disappeared into the woods.

There I sat, fully outfitted in borrowed gear – from the hat on my head to the boots on my feet. Even my rifle, bullets, and dragging gear were borrowed. I sat there thinking, *If I had to buy all this stuff, I'd be in the poorhouse.* Another reason it would be my last year to hunt.

But something wasn't right. I felt nauseous. Suddenly I threw up. I had to leave my post to make my way back to camp, where I lay on the couch until the guys found me at noon. They were afraid I had died.

I was sure they'd give me the rest of the day off. Wrong. By 1:00pm, a pale version of me could be found sitting in solitude back at Ray's Rock.

This is the last time! I vowed to myself.

The next half-hour seemed like an eternity. Suddenly, I heard a muted rustling in the distance. I expected to see one of my friends. Instead, I saw four-point antlers and the stately animal that bore them.

An adrenaline rush steamed my glasses. I had no idea what to do. I couldn't see, and I had never shot a gun.

I can't screw this up, I mused as I awkwardly and slowly lifted the 30-30 rifle to my shoulder. *But this trembling's gonna do me in!*

With no scope, just open sites, I leaned against the rock and pulled the trigger. The deer jumped. A jumping deer usually means a strike, and down he went. Now I was really shaking.

Within minutes, the area was surrounded with my cheering buddies. They were ecstatic and so was I. Soon George Vargo said, "Watch me," as he gutted my deer. The guys escorted me back to camp while *they* dragged the deer.

When I got home that night, with a deer on the roof rack of my car, my little boys, Jason and Jared, were wide-eyed with amazement. They were so proud of their dad. I made up my mind right then. *I'll be back for another round next year.* The hunting bug had bit me.

Immediately I began to buy hunting gear on the discount racks. I got a rifle for Christmas. I couldn't wait for the next year to come.

For some reason, I thought every hunting season would be like my first one. But three years went by without bagging a buck. I wouldn't be dissuaded. I read up on hunting, went to some seminars, and talked to experienced hunters. Yet, I was still very green.

My father-in-law, Jack Simmons, started to hunt with me. He was green, too. On opening day, he'd be up early for a shower. Then he'd douse himself with Old Spice cologne. I knew I'd be staying away from him in the woods!

One can only take so many years without some kind of success. When someone told me to go to the sports store for some buck lure, I was convinced *that* would be the ticket. Buck lure, a short wait in the woods, and the deer would be lining up. I thought, *This might be one of the best investments I've made so far.* I went home with the bottle that would make my hunting season.

It was early morning of opening day. I was dressed for sport and ready to enter the woods. There was only one thing left to do – apply the buck lure. Sometimes it doesn't matter if you read directions. Sometimes it does. This was one of the times it mattered.

I screwed off the lid. A rancid odor beyond belief permeated the air. I thought to myself, *Why would anyone use this stuff? But I'm a neophyte. Let's get on with it.*

I tipped the bottle so liquid would cover my fingers. I could hardly take the smell of buck urine, mixed with who knows what else. But I continued to gently pour the unpleasant liquid and apply it to my feet, knees, waist, chest, and hat. Almost unable to breathe, I ventured towards the woods.

I couldn't take it. After a short distance, I turned back to the house to de-scent myself, only to discover it was next to impossible to get the scent off my clothes. Once I could breathe a little better, I checked the directions.

Place cotton balls in 35mm camera film canisters and douse with buck lure. Then place in a circular pattern around your stand some 20 yards away.

One of my stellar hunting days it was not. My father-in-law ribbed me by saying, "Maybe you'll prefer my cologne to yours next time."

We made an agreement: neither of us would use our "cologne" again to go hunting.

19

OPENING DAY

From her youth on up, my wife Marie enjoyed gun target practice. So, after several years of just me hunting, she decided to join me in the woods. Turns out that she was a crack shot. On opening day of her first year, I was with her in the tree stand. She took down a deer in full flight. I still can't figure out how she did it.

Before long, Marie was a serious hunter. She was determined to do everything in her power not to be denied. She liked this one particular stand because she found it to be a producer. The only problem? The ladder steps up the tree were almost too far apart for her leg reach. She struggled to go up and down. But she figured, *Once up, it'll be worth it.*

Opening day came, and she was determined to get into that stand and take her deer. Just once up and she'd be set. She struggled to the top and set herself. The wind was formidable.

We would stay in contact by walkie-talkie. But she soon discovered hers had quit working. In the cold, she struggled to replace the batteries when one fell to the ground. That meant a trip down and up the ladder. She wasn't happy, but she had little choice.

Once back in the stand, it was time to hunt. She settled in. But before long, she had to pee. That meant another trip down and up. She was beyond annoyed. But down the ladder and up again she went. Now to the hunt.

A gust of wind assailed the tree. She reached for her rifle, but it eluded her and fell twelve feet to the ground below. When my walkie-talkie went off, I knew my hunter wife wasn't happy. It meant another trip down and up.

She told me about the trifecta. I thought it was hilarious, but I knew it would be a big mistake to let her know.

I came off my stand to hers. I assessed the damage: rifle okay, scope broken, wife upset. I tie-wrapped the scope to the barrel of the rifle but the hunt was over for the day. It's strange how misfortunes can strike one person funny and another person intensely aggravating. Marie was finally able to laugh at the end of the day.

* * *

On another opening day, we were each in our favorite stands as light dawned – Marie, her father, and I. Understand that we were on her father's 62-acre farm and spread out in the woods. Things were quiet as we were waiting for deer to appear.

But at 8:30am, a crew of four or five invading hunters went through the center of Dad's property hollering at the top of their lungs and banging sticks on buckets.

Dad was incensed. He hollered beyond what I thought was humanly possible, "Stop the racket and get off my land!" He repeated it several times. Marie heard the shout in the south and I in the west. There was no way we should have been able to hear him. His volume rivaled a rock concert's sound system. We couldn't stop laughing all day.

* * *

How about another opening day? Marie and I were on the front porch of her dad's country home. We were making our last-minute adjustments to enter the woods. It was 6:40am. You shouldn't hear shots until about 6:55am, but we did. Marie's bullet chamber jammed. She pointed her gun skyward and yanked on the lever.

BANG.

It was a super surprise for all of us. Marie had left a permanent branding on the house – a bullet hole through the porch roof.

I went into the house to inform her father. He asked if she wanted a knife to gut the roof. It was a good thing he thought it was funny.

* * *

One thing you hope for is that your kids will take up the sport. We took our boys hunting but they were reluctant. They hoped for the harvest, but they didn't enjoy the elements and the wait. They preferred their indoor video games.

Schools are closed in Pennsylvania on opening day of buck season. This particular year, we took two of our boys to Dad's farm and put them in good producing stands. Marie's stand was within eyesight of Jared's and Jason's within eyesight of mine.

Suddenly, Marie saw three deer in the distance walking east of her stand, headed directly for Jared's. She looked in his direction expecting him to be on red alert with rifle trained. Instead, there he lay on his back, fast asleep as the deer silently passed by. A perfect illustration of *You snooze, you lose.*

* * *

On a more recent opening day, I had to go to the bathroom. I waited as long as I could. It should have been quick and routine – unzip and go.

But it was unzip and no go. I fumbled around for a good half minute trying to find my long john's fly. It wasn't there! I had put them on backwards. Undressing in the cold, snowy woods was anything but fun. But I pictured me standing 10 feet away watching myself during the ordeal, and I couldn't help but laugh.

* * *

The years went by, and my father-in-law got too old to hunt. Marie gets too cold to hunt. So I go out by myself these days on opening day. I figure that I've earned the easy way to hunt – into the woods at 10:00am and out of the woods by 3:00pm in good weather. No more ungodly morning hours in all kinds of bad weather for me. But with just me hunting, there's not much to laugh about.

20

FORE!

If you play golf with me, you might get injured. You definitely need health insurance. That's because, on the golf course, *I'm* the ultimate hazard. I have absolutely no control over my shots. Someone said that I play military golf – left, right, left, right. But it's that occasional great shot that keeps me coming back. Sad to say, I've gotten close, but I've never broken 100. If I ever do, I'll throw a major party.

Most of my golf is with my son, my sister, my brother-in-law, and my colleagues at work. These are people who love me and who will usually extend me some grace.

My brother-in-law, Glenn Halteman, thought he knew how to stay out of my way. Once, after a decent shot, he drove me to my ball. Careful to stay in the cart, he sat completely even with me and to my right.

I pulled out my 5-iron, positioned myself, and swung away. Next thing I knew, I heard a scream and the rattling around of a golf ball. I had sliced the ball to my extreme right. Glenn dove for cover as the ball ricocheted inside his cart. These days, he gets behind me.

* * *

One summer, we had a youth intern at our church, Derek Sanford. He eventually followed me as Lead Pastor at Grace Church. He was a great athlete, and I decided to impress him by taking him golfing. He was soon to find out just how much I didn't know about golf.

Things went well for the first three holes. On Hole Four, we hit our balls off the tee. When we caught up with them, two greens were visible. One was straight ahead, and one was to our left.

"Derek," I said with confidence, "it's the green to the left. The one straight ahead is on another fairway."

We took our shots, only to hear objections from the twosome in front of us. "You're on the wrong green!" I sheepishly retrieved my ball and we shot toward the correct green.

The next hole was a defining moment for my ignorance. We got to the tee box. You could look in both directions and see fairways and flags. One flag was somewhat close. The other was far in the distance.

As we stepped into the tee-box, I announced, "See that flag way out in the distance? That's our hole. The other flag is just too close." Derek didn't question me. It was his first time on the course. Plus, I was his boss.

He hit his ball and I followed suit. Next thing I know, the same twosome ahead of us shouted again from a little distance beyond us. "What the heck are you doing? That's *our* hole! We're getting out of here before you kill us." I checked the tee-box sign, and sure enough, we had teed off backwards. Needless to say, I didn't positively impress Derek that afternoon. He laughed but said nothing.

* * *

On another occasion, several staff members and I were playing nine holes on a small country course. The fairway for the sixth hole was bordered by an electric fence all the way down to the green. The pasture on the other side was dotted with cattle lazily basking in the sun.

I gotta hit this ball straight, I mused. *I'll never find it if l hit it into the meadow.*

I fired off my shot. Sure enough, it veered to the left and across the electric fence where three cows lay napping in a little cluster.

Even from that distance, I heard the thud, followed by the bellowing "moo" from one of the cows. My ball had clunked him right on the shoulder. He rose from a lying to a standing position, faster than any cow I'd ever seen, as he surveyed me with a wary eye.

Instead of a "birdie" that day, I invented the "cowie."

* * *

But the pinnacle of all my errant shots happened with my son at a resort in Williamsburg, Virginia. We were on the first hole, and way in the distance stood two women on the green. Jared and I both realized that we could now shoot; we'd never interfere with their game.

We took our shots and mine didn't go very far. The ladies ahead of us finished and put up their flag, heading slightly in our direction as they walked towards their cart. Confident I could never hit a ball that far, I positioned myself with my 3-iron.

Click! It was an incredible shot: straight, far, and a little to the right. Next thing I know, one of the ladies winced and hollered. I had hit her square in the left breast! As she clutched herself, she glared in our direction. And then, throwing her hands into the air, she began screaming at me.

Her next action was priceless. She dropped my ball on the ground like one does when taking a penalty stroke. With a determined swing, she sent my ball soaring into the woods, gone for good. Then she looked in my direction and planted her feet. I knew she wasn't going anywhere.

Decision time. Do I move in her direction or return to the clubhouse?

Face the music, I said to myself as I began to prepare a little speech in my head. I was going to be effusive with my apologies. It would all work out. She'd forgive me.

Wrong. She held her ground as we approached. Before I could say a word, she addressed me like an angry drill sergeant before a delinquent recruit. And then she grimaced as she pointed to where I hit her, saying, "You hit me right here!" I apologized all over myself, but she wouldn't accept it.

Then she said these words that only an angry and delirious person would say after getting plunked by a novice like me. "We were going to let you play through. But now you'll follow behind us for the rest of the course!"

Instantly I thought, *Lady, if I hit you once, wouldn't you want us to play through and remove the danger?* Nope. She wanted to exact what she considered to be an appropriate form of punishment.

The fairway of Hole Five went in one direction. A grove of trees bordered it to the left. Hole Six came back in the opposite direction in parallel fashion. The same ladies were on the fairway on Hole Six. I teed off on Hole Five. Sure enough, my ball rattled around in the trees to my left and plopped onto their fairway.

No harm was done but I heard an angry screech and some choice words. I decided not to retrieve my ball and placed another one in our fairway. The penalty stroke was worth it because I knew better than to tangle with her again. That was the last we saw of them.

I confessed to Jared that I was exceedingly glad not to be that lady's husband. To which he said, "And she's exceedingly glad not to be your wife."

And that shot to the chest? The odds were so great against me hitting her that it was the equivalent to a hole in one.

21

THE HANG-UP

My father-in-law, John Simmons, and I have different philosophies about how to use a phone. It's been that way for over 50 years. When my phone rings, I answer it. When his home phone rings, he doesn't. He lets it go to voice mail and then he *might* answer once he hears who's calling.

A cell phone is part of my lifestyle. Not for him. He lives alone and loves to take long drives, sometimes to other states. I give him credit – he's 92. But no cell phone. He works in the yard for long seasons of time. No cell phone. There are many times we try to contact him over extended periods of time with no luck. No cell phone. Sometimes we worry. Sometimes we're peeved.

Our phone relationship predates the cell phone. We go back to the days of a phone hardwired to the house with the receiver on the end of a coiled cord. It was hard to get ahold of him then as well. He was a single man who lived in Peoria, Illinois, while we lived in Pennsylvania. Catching him near a phone or having him answer it was a crapshoot.

Are you getting the idea that the telephone isn't a major part of his world?

Maybe it's because he was a policeman for 23 years. The phone was a constant part of his job. So was his police car radio. There was constant phone or radio activity coming at him from all sides. Maybe he developed an aversion to telephones. Maybe that's why his daughter, my wife, isn't a fan of the phone either.

One thing Dad hates is receiving prank calls. But he's not averse to making them. He'd say, "Do you have Prince Albert in a can? You'd better let him out." Or, "Is your refrigerator running? You'd better catch it." And then he'd hang up.

But his getting a prank call was another story. If someone pranked him, down went the receiver and the phone wouldn't be answered for who knows how long. Sometimes I was the prank caller.

The most classic prank call I made to him happened like this. We were living in Erie, and he in a remote cabin some 30 miles from Peoria. Something urgent came up and I needed to call him. I was so glad that he finally answered the phone. I had tried to call him multiple times without success.

"Hello," he said. There was no premeditation on my part but, out of the blue, I instantly replied in a falsetto voice, "Hi. This is your girlfriend." The next thing I heard was a click and a dial tone. I kept saying, "Hello! Hello! This is Al. This is Al!" But it was too late.

I needed to talk with him. It was urgent. So I immediately called back. (This was before the days of the answering machine.) I let it ring and ring and ring. No answer. I'd wait a few minutes and try again and again and again. I knew he was there.

It was a Saturday morning and it continued like this intermittently throughout the day. I'm thinking, "He's got to know someone's really trying to get him." And he's thinking, "That prank caller won't give up! If he thinks I'm answering the phone, he can fly a kite."

Towards evening, I was getting very annoyed. "Darn it," I told Marie, "I had him on the phone and now he won't answer it. I need to talk with him! Now there's absolutely no way to contact him."

The same thing happened on Sunday. I tried to call him at intervals all day long. No answer. The same thing on Monday. I was getting a little hot under the collar. It had been three days!

Finally, on Monday night he answered the phone. We had quite a little exchange. It featured a lecture from me for not answering the phone and a defense from him about not answering prank calls. After we got that settled, I finally had that urgent conversation.

For the past 18 years, Dad has lived in Erie. We're just minutes apart. Unfortunately, his old phone habits still persist. But these days, I'm not afraid to prank call my father-in-law because I know that if he doesn't answer the phone, I can drive two miles and knock on his door.

But darn it. When I call him and he won't answer, it bugs the heck out of me. He won't budge!

Years ago when the phone rang, Dad often had a standard greeting. With no idea who was on the other end of the line, he'd say, "Hello, Murphy's Morgue. You stab 'em, we slab 'em. Wanna try our layaway plan?" With the advent of caller ID, those greetings are over.

But when I see him calling me on caller ID, my frequent greeting is still in a female voice, "Hi! This is your girlfriend." He doesn't hang up and we remember the first time that happened. And we both laugh.

Postscript:
Dad Simmons went to be with the Lord in May of 2021 at age 93.

22

THE WEDGIE

Camping and hiking have always appealed to me. But I've never been a fearless, push the envelope kind of guy. I've ruled out bungee jumping, parachuting, even skateboards. Parasailing is borderline.

When Marie's and my circle of friends decided to go whitewater rafting, it gave me pause. But heck, they were all in, including the wives. My apprehensions would stay hidden because there was no need to take a lot of kidding.

The weekend finally came. It was off to the Youghiogheny River in Ohiopyle, Pennsylvania. We rented a house in which we'd all stay on Friday night. There would be games, food, chatting, and lots of laughter.

Saturday morning came, and the weather was great. But the water was high in the river, making the Class III and IV rapids even more challenging. I didn't like the sound of it, but I wasn't about to say so.

We arrived at the rafting berth. Was I the only one with misgivings? I put them aside as the guide began to speak. He gave us a mini-seminar on the fundamentals of rafting and safety. Because the water was high, he was very specific and emphatic. He had my attention.

He instructed us on what to do if someone went overboard. He talked about several kinds of retrieval-into-the-raft techniques. He saved the most desperate for last. "If all else fails," he said, "throw modesty to the wind. Grab the person's swim trunks and give them the wedgie of their life. I can assure you, you'll get them back into the raft, and they'll thank you for it."

We had more in our party than one raft could hold, so the guide split us up into two rafts. He said a few parting words and launched our raft. He'd be in the other one.

We entered the gurgling Youghiogheny. The view was spectacular. The water was cold and agitated. I thought, *I'm staying low in this raft. Ain't no way I'm going overboard!*

The raft rose and fell. It spun around. It tottered from side to side. Up ahead was a mini-falls we'd have to traverse. There was no turning back. We were doing remarkably well. My confidence grew, but I still had a bravery deficit.

Our friends in the other raft were having way too much fun. But some other rafts weren't faring so well – people overboard. Things got scary from time to time, but no one in our raft panicked and no one went overboard. We were getting used to the river, and I was beginning to relax.

Until the guide shouted, "A major drop is coming. At the bottom is a big hydraulic. Be careful. Brace yourself. If someone goes overboard, you know what to do." I'm thinking, *I can't believe I signed up for this!* But there was only one option – take the plunge and hope for the best.

We descended the falls like pros. I was surprised but pleased. Of course, I stayed very low in the raft. We hit the hydraulic and it was like an agitator in an old washing machine gone wild. It spun us around. It spit at us. It rocked us like a roller coaster. It held us captive in its clutches, and then it suddenly released us to continue our journey.

But wouldn't you know it? Just as we came out of the hydraulic, Betty Korrell sat up and fell overboard. She was spinning around, blanketed by foaming water, and shouting, "Somebody, get me back in the raft!"

I was closest as we paddled toward her. I tried every technique I could remember to get her back into the raft, but it was as though she was coated with the slipperiest oil ever produced. I'd get her close, then she'd slip away.

She was getting a little more desperate, "Somebody! Get me into the raft!"

My thought from the start was, *This may require that last resort wedgie,* but I wanted to avoid it at all costs.

She slipped from my grasp again, and then again. Finally I announced, "Betty! Remember what the guide said? The wedgie as a last resort? I hate to do it, but here comes your wedgie. This is probably the only wedgie you'll ever get from a pastor." And with that, I reached down to her swimsuit bottoms and tightly grabbed all the material I could and pulled.

Amazingly, there was no slippage. She came over the side of the raft like a fish secured in a fisherman's net. Betty was finally in the raft. The wedgie was substantial, but she thanked me profusely.

I apologized. I told her that it was the last thing I wanted to do. But to her, it was all part of the rescue; no violation of personal space. I relaxed.

Just about that time, our raft entered a calm and serene portion of the river – no tempest, no froth, no roar. I took too much for granted and got higher in the raft than I should have. Before I knew it, *I* was overboard needing help to get back in. It was now *my* turn for a wedgie. And Betty's husband, Bill, happily obliged.

We have many exciting pictures and memories from that trip down the river. But there's no more compelling and riveting tale than the wedgie Betty sustained in rescue that day. In fact, she has recounted the story to her friends many times. She always concludes with these four words: "He saved my life!"

23

OLD YELLER

Walt Disney's *Old Yeller* hit the theaters on Christmas Day, 1957. It was an instant national success among children. Kids everywhere were singing the theme song, *The best doggone dog in the West.* I was in fourth grade.

To a kid, it seemed like the best movie ever made – out West, taming the land, two brothers, a dog, and adventure. The big word we all learned from the movie was "hydrophobia." It was an old word for rabies. If a dog got rabies, you had to "put him down."

That's exactly what happened to Old Yeller. He fought a rabid wolf and was bitten. As a precaution, they locked Old Yeller in a corn crib. Against hope, they waited to see if he had been infected. When his behavior turned nasty and he began to foam at the mouth, the older boy, Travis, had to put him down with his rifle.

Early on, Old Yeller was a nuisance and a pest to Travis. But eventually the dog won the hearts of the entire family. No one wanted him to die. Neither did we. We all cried. But Old Yeller had sired a pup who was mischievous like his father. "Young Yeller" eventually stole the hearts of the family, and he pretty much filled the hole left by Old Yeller.

Kids and dogs – a companionship like no other. But the story of Old

Yeller reminded all of us that one day, we'd have to say an emotional good-bye to a dear friend.

Tessie was the cutest little Pomeranian pup you ever saw. Our four kids took to her immediately. She was a very smart dog. She had a variety of barks, and we came to know what each one meant. Several school buses would pass our house every afternoon. Tessie knew which one our kids were on and out came the "bus bark." When she wanted popcorn, she'd let out the "popcorn bark" and lead us to the kitchen.

Tessie was only eight years old when she got sick. We took her to the vet. He said he could try to help her, but it would be quite expensive with no guarantees. He advised us to put Tessie down. We were broken-hearted.

"Do you want me to do it today?" asked the vet. "No," we replied. "Give us one more day to say our good-byes. We'll bring her back tomorrow." You can imagine the atmosphere around our house knowing the countdown was on.

Nightfall came. And that's when I hatched what I thought was a clever and consoling idea. *I'm going to help the family say good-bye to Tessie.* I gathered them in the family room with Tessie in our midst. I loaded the VHS tape and said, "We're going to watch Old Yeller. It'll help you say good-bye to Tessie."

Everyone hung in there as the movie played on. Then Old Yeller fought the wolf in the cornfield. The movie began to crescendo as it came time to say good-bye to Yeller.

At that point, something began to happen. My kids started to cry and, one by one, they left the room. No one would finish the movie. My attempt to prepare my kids for Tessie's farewell turned into a morbid failure. It wasn't the brightest idea I've ever had. But later, my kids forgave me because of my good intentions.

The next morning, Marie and the children took off with Tessie for the vet. I was too broken to go. The kids did better than I when that final hour came.

We laugh about it now. However, I learned a big lesson. Old Yeller isn't the movie to show your family when you have to say a final good-bye to your dog.

24

THE MARRIAGE RUBIK'S CUBE

A Rubik's Cube is a puzzle composed of a plastic cube containing multicolored movable smaller squares. The player attempts to twist and turn the little squares on each face of the cube until they're all the same color. It's an incredible, confusing challenge.

I liken the marital complexity in my extended family to a Rubik's Cube. There were lots of twists and turns so that understanding who and how people in the family are related to each other is a confusing challenge. I think you'll see what I mean.

My mother's sister, Millie Swartz, married a handsome young man by the name of John Mast from Delaware in 1957. I attended the wedding at the tender age of nine. I still have memories of the wedding and reception.

In the wedding party was a young lady by the name of Lillie Mast. She was John's sister, also from Delaware, and she was single. With that wedding, Lillie became Millie's sister-in-law. Even though I met Lillie there, she quickly became a distant memory. Kids rarely remember the strangers they meet if they never see them again.

The years went by. My parents, Al and Edith Detter, divorced in 1969. But my Dad still hung out at my mother's sister's place – at my Aunt

Millie's and Uncle John's.

In the intervening years, Lillie had taken a teaching job at Eastern Mennonite College in Harrisonburg, Virginia. One day, she came to visit Aunt Millie and Uncle John (her brother). My father, Al, happened to be at the house. Lillie and my dad met again, not having seen each other since John and Millie's wedding. They found themselves in the basement getting acquainted over a game of ping pong.

One thing led to another, and, in June of 1970, my Dad and Lillie married. I was the best man. Dad had married Millie's sister-in-law and John's sister. And Lillie, this complete stranger to me, became my step-mother.

And Aunt Millie and Uncle John? Aunt Millie (my mom's sister) was my Dad's sister-in-law and Uncle John (Millie's husband) was my Dad's brother-in-law while my Dad was married to my mother, Edith – his first marriage. Now, Aunt Millie and Uncle John were my Dad's sister-in-law and brother-in-law *again* because my Dad had just married Lillie, John's sister. And John and Millie, who were my uncle and aunt through my mother Edith, also became my step-uncle and step-aunt through Lillie, my new step-mother.

On August 1, 1970, Marie and I were married in Peoria, Illinois. My side of the family traveled from Pennsylvania to be there. Inclusive of the guests were my mother Edith, Uncle John and Aunt Millie, and my Dad and Lillie (my stepmother). How proud Marie's father, John Simmons, was to walk his daughter down the aisle. If he had a crystal ball to see the future that day, he wouldn't have believed it. None of us would have.

My new father-in-law, John Simmons, had been single since 1963 when Marie's parents divorced. He'd often visit our home in Erie, Pennsylvania, over the years. It wasn't unusual for my father-in-law, John, and my Dad and Lillie to visit our home in Erie at the same time. Over the years, Marie's Dad, my Dad, and Lillie became good friends.

On February 15, 1995, the phone rang. Tragic news awaited us. My father and his friend, Harry Kieber, had been killed in a car/truck accident. After the dust settled, my father-in-law (John), and Lillie (my late father's wife) began to notice each other. Things turned romantic, and, at Christmas that year, they called a family meeting. They announced their engagement and impending marriage.

Our children thought it was a joke. But they soon realized their Grandpa Simmons and Grandma Detter were serious. Our ten-year-old son, Ben, remarked, "I don't think Grandpa Detter would like this very much!" We all chuckled.

In April of 1996, I performed a wedding in the Erie church I pastored. I married my father-in-law, John, to widow Lillie (my dad's 2nd wife). Lillie went from being my step-mother to being my step-mother-in-law and from being my wife Marie's step-mother-in-law to being her step-mother. I had to wonder if somehow Marie had become my step-sister.

The guests laughed as I played with these family changes in my wedding talk. People had to really concentrate to understand the new relationships. At the reception, someone honored the complexity of the situation with the song, *I Am My Own Grandpa*.

You can solve this marital Rubik's Cube if you pay careful attention. But the best thing to do is to wait until Heaven. Relationships will be simple there. Jesus said, "They will neither marry nor be given in marriage; they will be like the angels in Heaven."

Yes, it will be much easier to figure out relationships in Heaven – there will only be sons and daughters of God and brothers and sisters in Christ. Lillie, for instance, awaits me in Heaven. She'll have gone from being my step-mother to being my step-mother-in-law to being my spiritual sister. That's a much simpler Rubik's Cube!

Marriage #1

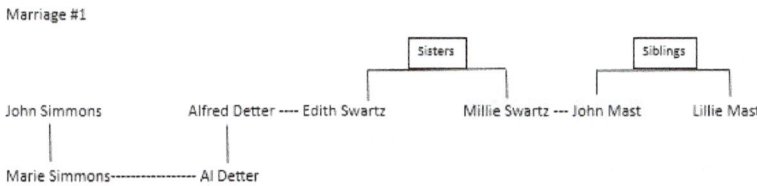

This marriage makes John Mast my uncle (as he married my aunt Millie) and makes Lillie Mast my Aunt Millie's sister-in-law.

Marriage #2

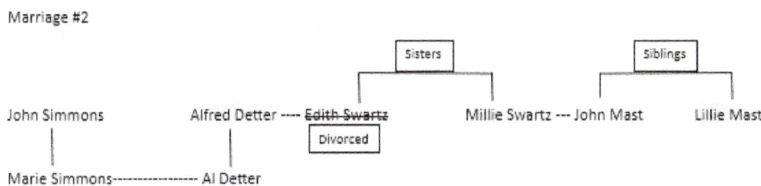

This marriage makes Lillie my step-mother by marrying my dad. My dad (already Millie's brother-in-law through his first marriage to Edith) becomes Millie's brother-in-law again through his marriage to Lillie (because his new wife, Lillie, is already Millie's sister-in-law). The same holds true for my Uncle John (becomes my dad's brother-in-law for a second time). Finally, my aunt Millie became the sister-in-law of my new step-mother (making her my step-aunt) and Uncle John now becomes my step-uncle (brother to my new step-mother).

Marriage #3

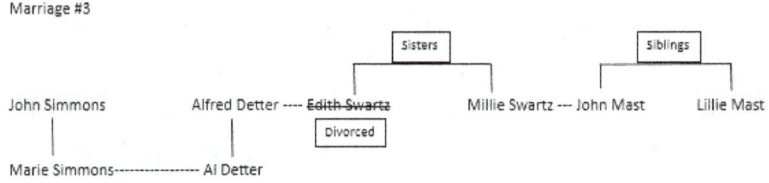

This marriage takes Lillie from being my step-mother (my father's wife) to being my father-in-law's wife. This makes her my wife's step-mother (and my step-mother-in-law). Keep in mind, before this marriage, Lillie was already my wife's step-mother-in-law through her marriage to my dad.

The Marriage Rubik's Cube Chart

25

TURFING

A definition for "turfing," the way I'm using it, is not in the dictionary. I checked. I'm tempted to send Merriam-Webster this definition: "Turfing is the act of driving through a person's yard, leaving behind ruinous ruts in the lawn."

I don't know how popular turfing is in other areas of the country, but it's been ridiculously common in Erie, Pennsylvania.

I first encountered turfing when we bought our house in the late 1970s. In the front yard was a semicircle of parallel tire tracks deep in the sod. The sellers graciously paid to fix it and I thought nothing more about it.

Until it happened again. And again. And again.

Repeatedly repairing my yard from turfing damage began to test my attitude. But I wasn't the only one. Multiple yards in the area suffered the same fate. Every so often, you'd find a car stuck in the muddy turf. There was a sense of satisfaction to know that the perpetrator got a fine and a bill for repairs.

One day I was getting my mail at our street-side mailbox. The neighbor kids were across the street. In broad daylight, a car squealed around the corner and careened though my yard. I dove for life-preserving cover as the car wiped out my mailbox and nearly ran over the kids. We were able to stop the car. The driver was a drunken groomsman after a wedding reception.

It finally dawned on me - *protect yourself and make them pay. They can't get away with this!*

I began collecting boulders the size of large buckets, spacing them so as to snag any careless violators. This method of prevention was largely successful. Every so often, a car would enter my yard and tangle with those rocks. Sometimes they escaped. Sometimes they didn't.

These turfing events usually occurred between 11:00pm and midnight. We'd be in bed when we'd hear the screeching of tires turning the corner, the spinning of sod, and the clanging of metal against the rocks. I'd get a twinge in my stomach, and my primal instincts would take over. It was time to race downstairs and into the street, regardless of my state of dress. To hesitate an instant might mean losing the perpetrator.

One night I was in the shower. The familiar sound of turfing greeted my ears. My adrenaline took over. I only had time to grab my bathrobe. Drenching wet, in my bare feet, and naked underneath my robe, I flew down the stairs and into the street. There was the car, hung up over a rock. Marie was right behind me, both to call the police and to be sure that I wasn't like Joseph in the Old Testament or Peter in the New. Both lost their robes.

Now, understand what happens to a person when the turfing incidents pile up over the years. With each new incident, there's a whole, pent-up history that accompanies it. You move to red alert and spontaneous action. Enough is enough. You must catch the culprit at any cost.

And so it was that, one Saturday night, I was in bed when I heard the haunting noise of turfing, minus the rocks. I couldn't figure out what was happening until I looked out my back bedroom window. There was a guy driving through my backyard! His only exit was to back out and I knew I only had precious seconds if I was going to apprehend him.

I bounded down the stairs and made a beeline to the backyard. By that time, the renegade car was out of my yard, fleeing down the street. Alas, it was a lost cause.

One of the neighbors was already at the scene. Bill Detisch and I reviewed the damage together. It was easy to see under the brightness of the streetlight. We talked about some of the more memorable previous instances of turfing in the neighborhood.

Then, with a grin on his face and a twinkle in his eye, he said, "Pastor, do you realize that you're standing before me in just your underpants?" I was on a not-to-be denied mission and I never gave it a thought. I flushed with embarrassment and said, "See you later," vanishing into the darkness as quickly as I could. All Marie could do was shake her head.

The next morning, in the Sunday School class I was teaching, I told the story to uncontrollable laughter among my students. They never did remember the lesson I came prepared to give. The one they remembered was, *Always get dressed before you leave your house.*

Turfing in recent years has subsided substantially. But now I have easy-to-get-into clothes and bedroom slippers ready just in case.

26

THE SMILE

The unthinkable happened in November of 1996. Our doorbell rang at six in the morning. When we opened the door, two solemn police officers were standing on our front porch.

"Do you have a son named Jason?" they asked. We answered that we did. They continued, "You need to go to Hamot Hospital immediately and make a positive identification."

Marie began to cry, and, in weakness, I fell to the floor in a kneeling position. As a pastor for decades, I knew what policemen at the door meant.

"Is he alive?" I whispered.

"We can't give you that information. All we can say is that he was alive at the scene." They offered a word of comfort, and then they were gone.

In disbelief, we woke our other three children and threw on some clothes. I cried out the same prayer the entire 10-minute ride to the hospital, "Lord, if You've called Jason home, we release him. If he's still alive, please spare his life!"

I never expected to see him alive again.

We were immediately escorted into the emergency room. For a

second, we had no idea who the form was on the gurney because of the spaghetti network of wires and tubes surrounded by a collection of noisy monitors. We stepped closer for a good, unobstructed look. Our fears were confirmed. The motionless man in the bed was our 19 year-old son.

I could barely speak the only question relevant to the circumstances, "Is he alive?"

"Yes," came the reply and a tentative hope was born within my soul.

"Will he survive?"

"It's touch and go," a doctor said. "He's in a coma, and the next 72 hours will be critical."

We'd never been near a traumatic brain injury (TBI) before. We had no idea about the journey that would lay head: nineteen days in a coma in the hospital, five months in a rehab facility, and endless doctors and therapists thereafter.

The day Jason entered the rehab hospital, we met with the staff. It wasn't good news.

"Your son will never be the same. He may always be in a vegetative state." They were trying to prepare us for a new reality and worst-case scenario. We were crushed.

Meanwhile, Jason was on the third floor, unaware of his surroundings: bed-bound, eyes closed, in diapers, unable to speak, completely incapacitated. We stood vigil at his bedside every day. We followed him to therapy. Steady streams of people came to encourage us. Each day seemed like an eternity.

Eventually one eye opened; days later the other. But any eye contact was empty of connection. Then some movement of his arms and legs began to occur. With each little improvement, it was like cheering when your baby begins to crawl or say his first words.

But there were no words from Jason and absolutely no conversation. I developed a daily routine. I'd walk into his room and greet him.

Taking his hand I'd say, "Hi Jason, if you know who I am, squeeze my hand."

Nothing. Every day I persisted, and every day, nothing.

When I came into his room the week before Christmas, I could sense something was different, even though I didn't know what it was. I again took his hand and said, "Jason, if you know who I am, squeeze my hand."

This time he looked at me. And he spoke! Just two words, "Pastor Al." The people in the room exploded with joy. It wouldn't surprise me if the noise had rocked the whole hospital.

From that day forward, there was a little more eye contact, a few more words, sitting up in a chair, drooling down his chin, resisting his trach. A normal life for Jason was light years away, if at all. But we decided to rejoice at each and every improvement.

We had little to laugh about. But there were times we couldn't chase the laughter away. Like the time "Uncle" Buck came to visit him. Jason coughed and launched a glob of phlegm that landed squarely on Buck's forehead. Yes, it was gross. But it broke the bubble of tension. We couldn't stop laughing. Jason remained as serious as a judge.

The hospital staff warned us that, as brain-injured patients recover, they often use profanity: "Even the Pope would do it if it happened to him," they said.

One day, I stood at the foot of Jason's bed and asked him a question. He looked at me and dropped the F-bomb in a two-word sentence. I did something I never thought I'd do over profanity. I cheered, "Yes! He spoke!" And I continued, *"Any* word he says is exciting!"

Christmas Day arrived and, at six in the morning, we got a phone call from the rehab hospital. Jason had had an incident. It wasn't good. We rushed to his side.

By evening, things were under control so we had our Christmas in his room with family and close friends. It was such a mixture of sorrow and renewed hope.

There was laughter in the room, but not from Jason. It was like someone had stolen his ability to laugh. We helped him open gifts. It was all very mechanical. Finally, someone gave him a baseball cap. It sat there on his lap until someone put it on his head. He promptly grabbed the bill and threw it on the floor. It was progress and everyone laughed!

Everyone but Jason.

Now understand, Jason had been a virtual laughing machine before his accident. He loved humor and he loved comedy. His laugh was contagious. Now, it was completely gone. How we missed it! We tried to get it back. Along with encouraging him in therapy, inducing him to laugh was our mission.

When family and friends came to visit, we made it our goal to tell silly jokes. We made faces. We recounted funny memories. We played some of his favorite comedians like Jeff Foxworthy. It was a total dead battery. He was deadpan-faced. There wasn't a trace of laughter in his being.

Still we persevered.

Toward the end of January, one of Jason's friends said something funny during a visit. Incredibly, a smile spread across Jason's face, followed by a chuckle and then full laughter. It was like someone had flipped a switch. From that moment forward, Jason was able to laugh. And laugh he did. I went home that night and wrote a touching poem about Jason's moment of laughter called "The Smile."

Everyone was thrilled including the hospital staff. He even started to make *them* laugh. Except for one occurrence when Jason was getting mobile in his wheelchair. He raided the lounge refrigerator of its chocolate pudding. The nurse got cranky about it.

But Jason thought it was funny.

Jason will always have some handicaps, but he has his laughter back. He's once again the laughing spark of any social gathering. If I had the opportunity to give Jason a second name, there'd only be one choice –

Isaac.

It's the Hebrew word for laughter.

POSTSCRIPT – THE POEM I WROTE: THE SMILE

His smile came so easy, he loved to laugh and play,
 But one day it was missing, at the close of a tragic day;
 It was stolen from him quickly, by a sly thief in the night,
 His eyes were closed in trauma, he could not see the light.

No smile was expected, as he lay there in his sleep,
 It was hidden deep within him, for the angels there to keep;
 In time he made improvements, he spoke, he ate, he sighed,
 But still he could not smile, no matter how he tried.

The signs of troubling passions, appeared upon his face,
 But the humor in his soul, had somehow been erased;
 The moments came upon him, to smirk or laugh or grin,
 But his face remained so sober, nothing welling from within.

What thief could be so ruthless, to lock his smile away?
 The thief of pain or injury, or depression of the day?
 No answer was forthcoming, we'd have to wait and see,
 How long it took, if ever, for him to show some glee.

And then one night it happened, while sitting in his chair,
 With friends and family gathered, just chatting with him there;
 We tried to coax a smile, to see if he would try,
 We told a funny story, but all he did was sigh.

When suddenly without warning, a shadow of a smile,
 All eyes began to stare at him, as though he were on trial;

It started as a grin, then flashed across his face,
Like the bursting of the sunlight, into a cloudy place.

We had waited for so long, we laughed and then we cried,
The value of a smile, just could not be denied;
The sparkle in his eyes, the gleam across his face,
Gave us hope and courage, to continue in the race.

27

FAMOUS PEOPLE

There's a desire in many of us to meet famous people. I'm no different.

I've been fortunate. I've met my share of people who have been in the spotlight. I had dinner with Dale Robertson in Chicago. He was the star of the old TV series, *Tales of Wells Fargo.* Movie star Charlton Heston of *Ben Hur* fame came to Erie for a National Rifle Association rally. I shook his hand.

Gospel singer George Beverly Shea sang at my college, the Moody Bible Institute, while I was a student. I waited in line to meet him after a service. On a plane from Cleveland to Los Angeles, I spotted E. V. Hill, a great black preacher from Los Angeles. He signed the flyleaf of my Bible.

I spent some time at a church in Fresno, California where Jim Maloney was on staff. He had been a star pitcher for the Cincinnati Reds. One night, I sat with Gus Zernial at a minor league baseball game in Fresno. He was the major league home-run champion in 1951, playing for the Kansas City Athletics. At a convention in Chicago, I met Jim Bunning. He pitched a perfect game against the Mets for the Phillies in 1964.

Marie and I were at the NCAA March Madness basketball tournament when Rick Fox played for North Carolina. Marie thought he was cute, so she asked for his autograph at the Newark airport. Going through the Pittsburgh airport on the way home, we spotted ice skating champion, Scott Hamilton. He was glad to give us his autograph. It was a privilege to meet Joe Paterno, head football coach of Penn State, when he came to Erie.

Moving to politics, I've met a number of household names. I had dinner with Pennsylvania Senator Rick Santorum at a banquet where I emceed. Former Pennsylvania Governor and Homeland Security Director Tom Ridge lived one mile from me in Erie. I'd see him around town. I met Bill O'Reilly, Laura Ingraham, Chris Wallace, and Charles Krauthammer when they came to Erie for a special engagement. Rudy Giuliani signed his picture on the cover of Time Magazine for me.

When former Vice President Dick and Lynne Cheney came to town, I met them. The biggest thrill of all was when Marie and I met former President George and Laura Bush. When he asked what I did, I told him that I was a pastor. He smiled with approval and told me, "Preach the Word."

But none of them were on my select dream list of two. I don't know why, but I knew that I'd be a fulfilled man if somehow, somewhere, some place, someday, I'd meet them. The names on that little list? Billy Graham and Tom Landry. I'd have traded meeting everyone else if I could but just meet those two.

The Urbana triennial missions conference for young adults met in the Illinois college town for which it was named. As part of my job with my denomination, I was among the 18,000 who attended. It was 1976. Billy Graham was on the program.

The afternoon he spoke, I showed up two hours early to get a front row seat. When he finished, the moderator said the magic words, "Billy Graham will remain on the platform and greet as many as he can."

In the middle of the closing prayer, I walked to the stage. It was waist high. Soon the area was mobbed. I was so pressed against the stage I couldn't move. The only question was, "Would he come in my direction?"

Billy moved to his right, away from me. Suddenly he reversed direction. I was going to meet Billy Graham! I grabbed my pen and business card. He shook my hand as he greeted me. I was ecstatic when he took my pen and signed my card. In a state of euphoria, I walked the several blocks to my hotel feeling like my feet never touched the ground.

A week or so later, my phone began to ring – at home and at my office. My friends were telling me the unbelievable. My picture was in at least eight news magazines around the country. The press had snapped a picture of Billy shaking my hand! That very moment had exploded into the recording of a dream come true.

There was one more name on my list – Tom Landry. Tom was the longtime coach of the Dallas Cowboys. He was a Christian, a man who walked the talk. And he was a darned good coach. We lived in Erie; he lived in Texas. How would I ever get to meet him?

In the summer of 1998, we loaded our van and our family took off on a 3-week trip out west. When we visited relatives in Austin, they weren't going to let us leave without some good, authentic Mexican food.

It was time to pay the bill. I moved toward the cash register when someone in my left peripheral vision caught my eye. It was a bald head and square jaw. You'd almost think it was Tom Landry. I stopped for a direct look.

Leaning over to my son Jared, I whispered, "Turn around and tell me who's sitting at that table!" He confirmed that it was Tom Landry. I said to myself, *This is the second half of my dream come true. Celebrities don't like to be disturbed in public. But if it's not now, it's never.* My family stood in place gawking as I approached his table.

"Mr. Landry," I said, "If you'll give me one second, I need to say something to you. I've had a dream of meeting you all my life. I know you probably don't like to be bothered." He looked up at me with a sober face.

I continued, "You're on the board of Dallas Seminary from which I'm a graduate." He showed a smile. "May I have your autograph?" There was nothing to write on, so I had to think fast, "How about your napkin?" He took my suggestion, signed his napkin, and I shook his hand.

I was ecstatic! When I left the restaurant, I kept shouting, "I can't believe it! I met Tom Landry!" I must have repeated that line 100 times while on the freeway going home. My oldest son Jason finally chimed in. (Two years earlier, he had been in a near fatal car/truck accident that left him with a traumatic brain injury. He had recovered quite a bit by this trip, including his sense of humor.)

"Hey, Dad."

I responded, "What, son?" He replied, "Do you love Tom Landry more than you love God?" The family exploded in laughter to the point that I could hardly drive. It was the funniest line of the whole trip.

I had finally met the two famous people that I always most wanted to meet. Why not laugh?

28

THE BEES

Bees and picnics are an unwelcome combination. Some years the bees are worse than others.

One summer the bees were almost like one of the plagues in Egypt. Every time we had a meal on our deck, squadrons of bees buzzed the table.

No one was ever stung, but the bees posed a psychological threat. And they were a downright mega-nuisance. We'd swat at them. We'd cover dishes. We'd yelp and jump if they got too close.

This invasion of bees was getting old. There was no relief in sight. All we wanted was to sit around the table and enjoy a meal. Wasn't gonna happen – not that summer.

I'm not an inventor. I'm not into construction. But I'm somewhat of the handyman type. I like to look at problems around the house and solve them. And when I do, I'm kind of proud of myself.

One of my specialties is thinking up clever solutions. Some solutions turn out to be next to genius. Others aren't so smart. My solution to the bee problem falls into the latter category.

One day I noticed how much the bees liked the barbecue sauce on the ribs. Dozens of them would hover over the sauce. This keen observation birthed an idea. At the time, I thought it was foolproof.

Into the kitchen I marched. I grabbed the jar of barbecue sauce and emptied it into a Styrofoam bowl. The next stop was the driveway, where I deposited the bowl. I figured this would be the feast the bees were looking for and it would summon all the renegade bees within a block of our house.

What these bees didn't know was that the executioner would be ready for them. I returned inside the house in search of our Electrolux vacuum sweeper.

Here was the theory. The bees would arrive at the sauce bowl by the droves. I'd stand near the bowl with the sweeper hose in hand, the motor running full bore. With the sucking power of our sweeper, the swarm of bees wouldn't have a chance. They'd be sucked into the sweeper bag, I'd tie a baggie over the opening on the hose, and my problem would be solved. I'd be rid of those unrelenting pests.

Unfortunately, I didn't consult my wife about the plan.

Out the garage door I came, sweeper in hand, confident that I had hatched a truly genius plan. As I approached the bowl of marinade, my hopes were high, for there was a congregation of bees buzzing the bowl. All I needed to do was to get the hose in the vicinity of those bees and the deed would be accomplished.

I flipped the switch, and the vacuum sweeper came to life. As I approached the bowl, the bees began to scatter. But there were a few brave ones hanging near the bowl, trying to get one last taste before they retreated. I lowered the hose toward the bowl to catch whatever bees I could.

It was then that the unexpected happened.

Instead of capturing any bees, the hose sucked the weightless bowl to its nozzle and there it stayed. I fumbled to find the off-switch, but the damage had been done. The sauce had journeyed its way through the hose and into the vacuum bag at a high rate of speed.

To say that I was shocked at the sudden turn of events would be an understatement. But more was to come.

Marie rounded the corner just in time to witness the experiment go south. She shrieked in disbelief, "No! What have you done to my vacuum sweeper?"

Somewhat tongue-tied, I tried to explain my plan and my logic. She wasn't having it. My "foolproof" solution to the bee problem revealed who the fool really was. At least that's what I think was going through Marie's perturbed mind.

She forgave me. The bees persisted around our meal table on the deck for the rest of the summer. And the vacuum sweeper? It wasn't damaged. But there was no way to totally clean out the hose. For the next three months, every time we ran the sweeper, it smelled like barbecue sauce in the house. And Marie would give me "the look."

I now run all my cleverly devised household solutions by Marie first.

29

NYLONS AND BRAS

No man should ever have to experience what I went through one Christmas. It started out innocently enough. But things got complicated.

After couples get married, the art of giving gifts to each other changes over the years. I didn't expect that it would, but it did.

In our early years, we had little money and very few things. The joy of getting something very surprising and exciting for each other at Christmas was a challenge we relished. We could hardly wait to give our gifts. In those early years, some friends who had been married over forty years said, "We don't give each other Christmas gifts anymore." They didn't elaborate, but I thought, *Are your middle names Scrooge?* It was years later that we began to understand what they meant.

The kids came along, four of them, and the excitement began to shift from giving gifts to each other to giving gifts that would make our children squeal with delight. But even then, Marie and I went to great lengths to find gifts that would joyfully surprise each other.

One Christmas, I bought Marie a gift that would be impossible to guess. It was an antique sculpture by John Rogers, called *The Charity Patient,* portraying a doctor helping a baby in the arms of an indigent mother. It was heavy and sizable. I wrapped it and, when I gave it to her, Marie thought it was a box of bricks. Her eyes widened with disbelief and delight as she beheld her unexpected surprise.

The years went by, and we had enough "stuff." It became harder to buy gifts for each other. We'd make our lists, but the requests became increasingly practical: socks, a belt, slacks, jeans.

A seminar leader on marriage once said, "Be sure that you don't buy your wife anything for Christmas that has a plug on it." So, I always ruled out toasters, electric frying pans, hair dryers, and the like. And I knew that a Chia pet would never ingratiate me to Marie.

One year, there wasn't much on our lists so I included undershirts and underpants, with sizes, on mine. Following my example, Marie put nylons and bras on her list, along with the sizes. It looked pretty straight-forward. Until I went shopping for them.

You see, buying underpants and undershirts for a man is easy. You look for the best price on Fruit of the Loom or Hanes at Walmart. You have a choice between briefs or boxer underpants, and crew neck or V-neck undershirts. No need for designer underwear; just get a multi-pack with an extra free pair. And make sure they're tagless for less irritation. Marie would be in and out of the men's department in just a few minutes.

I was soon to learn it wouldn't be that easy for me.

Off to the mall I went. I immediately felt uncomfortable, for I was the lone man in the lingerie section of the department store.

I looked for the nylons first. I knew the size she wanted, but I wasn't prepared for the plethora of options. There were all kinds of brands. There were options for the legs from the ankles all the way to pantyhose. There were more color choices than a rainbow. There were lettered size-charts, open toes, closed toes, nude toes, reinforced toes, not to mention the heel options. I was in a quandary. I felt helpless.

I migrated to the bra section. Certainly, *that* had to be easier. I had the size. Just go pick up a three-pack. But the bra department turned out to be worse than the nylons department, for I found that "size" was not the only issue. There were options of every sort, options that I didn't know existed: underwire, wire-free, adjustable straps, non-adjustable straps, front close, back close, unlined, lined, push-up, X-back, H-back, polyester, cotton, Spandex, knit, and capital letters for sizes that spanned most of the alphabet. I wondered if there were engineering departments at bra factories.

Beads of sweat broke out on my forehead.

I had absolutely no clue what to buy. I just knew that I wasn't going home empty-handed. I screwed up some courage and went to the lady clerk.

"Uh, could you please help me? I'm buying my wife some Christmas presents, and I've never been alone in this department before."

She looked incredulous and must have been thinking, *You've got to be kidding. You're buying intimate apparel for your wife for Christmas?*

I showed her the size on my list and said, "My wife is 5'3" and 120 pounds. She's attractive and this will be a surprise for her. If you were me, what would you buy her? I've never seen so many choices."

She didn't realize that I had already perused all the options, so she went through them all again while my eyes glazed over.

Then she said, "Every lady is different, and I have no clue what your wife would want. Maybe you should ask her and come back."

Ask her and come back? Not on your life. This was going to be a Christmas gift and it had to be a surprise.

I made a decision. Find her size nylons and buy several pairs. Find her size bras and buy several. Don't worry about the options. Just pick some at random. Wrap them and hope for the best. If she doesn't like them, I'll get an "A" for effort, and she can exchange them at the store.

You should have seen the surprise on Marie's face when she opened her nylons and bras. "Oh, honey, you shouldn't have! They're really nice, but they're not what I wear. Do you mind if I exchange them?"

She was right about one thing when she said, "You shouldn't have." I retired from bra and nylons shopping that very moment. When we go to the mall now, we split up. Marie goes to the ladies' department and I to the men's.

Yes, shopping for each other has changed over the years. And perhaps the biggest surprise is this: after 50-plus years of marriage, we don't buy each other anything for Christmas. There's nothing we need.

But we have "Christmas" several times a year. When we're out, she'll buy me something nice and say, "That's for Christmas," and I'll do the same for her. And so here I sit writing this story at the desk Marie bought me for Christmas this past October. No more lists and no more having me shop for women's underwear.

Funny thing, Marie never did buy me any underwear that Christmas.

30

THE EXPENSIVE DINNER

Vacations at the shore were part of my life since preschool days. When my parents, sister, and I would visit relatives in Delaware in the 1950s, it was Rehoboth Beach. In the 1960s, it was Ocean City, New Jersey. We rented rooms in boarding houses near the boardwalk, nothing fancy.

Even though marriage took me to Chicago and Dallas, going to the Jersey Shore was always on the back burner. When our children came along, the tradition lived on. By then we resided in Erie, Pennsylvania, so trips to Ocean City happened almost annually.

The memories are rich and numerous: biking on the boardwalk early in the morning, the boardwalk amusement parks, miniature golf, swimming and sunbathing, shopping, fun food, people-watching, low-flying seagulls (one hitting me on the head and chest with its payload), and finding coins between the boardwalk slats. One year, our boys found over $50 – a lot of change for kids to spend while on a shore vacation.

Our kids left the nest and family beach vacations became sporadic. But that didn't mean Marie and I couldn't go as a couple. What about a destination other than Ocean City? Open for a new adventure, we decided on Hilton Head. We did some research and made our reservations.

Our departure date arrived, and we made our way to the airport. As is our custom, we went to the podium at the gate and said, "If you're overbooked, we're willing to be bumped. And if your cabin is full, we'd be happy to bump up to First Class." We have a little list of places we'd like to fly to but funds are limited. A little delay for free trips makes good math sense to us.

Wouldn't you know it? The economy seats were overbooked. The gate attendant approached me with a smile, "How'd you like a First-Class seat?" I gladly accepted. The only problem?

There was just one seat. I found my way there with delight.

The question came up later, "Why didn't you give the seat to Marie?" The simple answer, "We were so surprised, neither of us thought of it."

I had never flown First Class before. The food and service were superb. I was wondering how much extra it would have cost.

A gentleman was sitting to my right; I had the aisle seat. He was unusually friendly, and we struck up a conversation. He was a successful businessman from New England. He, his wife, and another couple were on their way to Hilton Head. It was a yearly thing for them. They'd be staying at the same plantation as we.

We talked like old friends for the rest of the flight, and we gave each other assurances that we'd get together several times during the week. We exchanged cell phone numbers and parted company.

The next day we encountered them on the beach. Vacation weeks can get quite busy, so we set a date for Thursday night – the six of us – for dinner.

Thursday night arrived, and we made our way to the restaurant. It was on the waterfront, and it looked high-end. It was. Reviewing the menu, Marie and I had instant sticker shock. There were only a few items in the upper twenties. From there it was $30, $40, and $50. Marie and I never have money like that to spend on dinner.

When you're married as long as we have been, you develop nonverbal body language for lots of things. That night, *Order the cheapest entree on the menu,* was our mutual message. We made our low end selections, and the waiter took our order.

The other couples ordered rather expensive meals. They added appetizers and alcoholic beverages, while we stayed with ice water and a lemon slice. Out came the appetizers. They looked so good, but we just watched. Shortly thereafter, the main entrees arrived – delightful to the eye, with generous, tasty portions. These people knew how to dine!

Following plenty of conversation laced with laughter, the main meal concluded and the waiter returned. The other two couples ordered coffee and dessert. We declined as the waiter poured us more water. By now, the tab was escalating. I was trying to calculate what theirs would cost. I had yet to add the tax and tips. Marie had already figured what our portion would be.

The desserts looked incredible as we looked on with 'sanctified' envy. Before long, we were finished, and it was time to leave. The waiter brought the bill.

It was on one check. We wondered, *Is one of these new friends picking up the tab?* Then the announcement was made, "We have a tradition when we go out to eat. We split the bill evenly among all the couples."

With that, the amount each of us was responsible for was revealed. Marie and I swallowed hard and communicated with our special nonverbal marital language, *Surely they're kidding!* They weren't. We had gone as cheaply as possible. And now we were funding their dinner all the way from appetizers to dessert. We were surprised, but we amicably paid our share.

As we returned to our villa, ordering lightly and splitting the bill was the topic of conversation. We realized that it was all innocent. We had dined with people in the business world who had means, and they never thought twice about their tradition.

As Marie and I closed the topic of conversation, we agreed that it wasn't just about the cost of the meal. It was an investment in making new friends. And it gave new meaning to the adage, "When in Rome, do as the Romans."

We did. Rome is expensive.

31

THE PYRAMID

A destination wedding. I've only ever performed one, but I can recommend them.

Some friends of ours, Matt Sahlmann and Beth Thornton, were in their late forties and wanted to have a wedding to remember – a special, private ceremony on the beach in Riviera Maya, Mexico. Matt extended the invitation, "Would you and Marie consider flying to Mexico to do our wedding? Everything will be paid for." Not one of the harder decisions of my life, I said yes almost instantly.

Everything was set when a major complication caught us by surprise. Our daughter Rachel was expecting, and the due date was five weeks past the wedding date. Nothing could go wrong, right?

Rachel was at work when her water broke the day before we were to fly out for the wedding. Our baby granddaughter, Alexis, was five weeks early and landed in intensive care.

I called Matt and Beth to explain the situation. They were more than gracious. But we had to create Plan B. We agreed to meet at Red Lobster, their favorite restaurant, at 4:00pm that day to problem-solve.

We arrived at a plan. They'd fly out on schedule the next morning. We'd fly down three days later, if Alexis stabilized, and do the wedding then.

But we thought of another problem – the bride and groom-to-be can't sleep together in Mexico if they're not married.

I was one step ahead of them. I had come to the restaurant ready to marry them – a brief ceremony to make it legal and then the special ceremony a few days later in Mexico. I had informed the obliging restaurant staff, and that's why I requested the remote table in the back corner of the restaurant.

The couple was glad I was ready to marry them, but the groom responded emphatically, "Absolutely not in Red Lobster!" So we finished dinner and went directly to the church I pastored at the time.

A 10-minute ceremony, and the deed was done. Away they went. None of us knew whether Marie and I would join them in Mexico in a few days.

But Alexis stabilized. We left for Mexico on Monday, and on Tuesday night, we had that special beach wedding.

After the wedding, the bride and groom invited us to journey 100 miles with them on a tour bus to the ruins of the ancient Mayan city, Chichen Itza. We accepted. Two days later, we boarded a bus for the two-hour trip. With great anticipation, we reached our destination.

There it stood – an imposing and magnificent pyramid – 10 stories high with staircases of 91 steps on all four sides. As I peered at the pyramid, I noticed that the steps and the top were covered with people. But I have a problem; I'm afraid of heights. I have dreams of being at the edge of a cliff ready to tumble over.

I began to debate about climbing the pyramid. I said to myself, *I don't think I want to.* But I also said, *This will be my one and only time to be here.* I decided to climb to the top.

Understand, there are no railings or safety features on the pyramid except one lonesome rope that lies on only one set of stairs from top to bottom. Of all things, I decided to climb a set of stairs that had no rope.

I thought, *I can do this!*

Starting out upright, I stepped briskly up the high steps. About three stories up, I looked behind me and froze. I felt an acute sense of fear, like I do in my dreams. The view looked like a vertical drop!

From that point on, it was a hand-and-knee, pyramid-hugging belly crawl to the top. I was determined to never look behind me again. Finally reaching the top, I crawled on my hands and knees to the temple wall about ten feet from the edge. Then I stood up and walked around all four sides of the little temple, touching the walls all the while, looking over the city ruins.

But curiosity began to overtake me. I thought, *I wonder what it looks like at the edge of the pyramid.* With a flash of bravery, I got on my hands and knees and crawled to the edge. Lying flat on my belly, I peered over the side. In an instant, I had enough and crawled, once again, to the safety of the temple wall.

Then something crossed my mind I hadn't thought of when deciding to climb the pyramid – *I'd have to come down.* Petrified, I thought about my options – stay on the top indefinitely or hire a helicopter to come get me. One or two more ideas crossed my mind. But the only one that made sense was to convince myself to go back down the stairs.

My body language screamed trepidation and fear to the point that one lady said to me, "Sir, are you okay?" When I said "Yes," I lied.

Finding the steps with the rope, I grabbed it and hung on as tightly as I could. I turned around backwards and slowly descended that pyramid – face and belly towards the steps, on my hands and knees, never looking behind me.

When I got to the bottom, I met my party who had already descended much more quickly than I and I bravely said, "Piece of cake!" But they all knew differently and told me so. They had pictures to prove it. I secretly decided never to climb something like that again.

But memories fade. Some years later, my family convinced me to climb Moro Rock with them in Sequoia National Park, California. It's extremely high and steep. My grandsons, Luke and Justus, scampered to the top like mountain goats. But as I got higher, I began to freak out, and the same feelings I'd had on that Mayan pyramid overwhelmed me.

I finished the climb on my tummy and, arriving at the top, I loudly proclaimed, "I'm the world's biggest sissy and I don't care who knows it! I've got to get down from here NOW!" Fear had overtaken me. Refusing to have my picture taken with my family, I descended Moro Rock like I did the pyramid. But there was no rope!

My family had a good-natured chuckle at the plight of its patriarch. But everyone knows with certainty – NEVER AGAIN!

32

THE NEEDLE-NATO UNIT

When my daughter, Rachel, was nineteen, she had her first baby five weeks early. It was touch and go. Rachel knew nothing about hospitals. All she knew was that Alexis was in intensive care in the neo-natal unit. Rachel heard the pronunciation as the "needle-nato" unit and that's what she said as she sent people to peer through the unit window to see Alexis.

Eight years later, the "needle-nato" unit became necessary again. Rachel was at work when she was stricken with unbearable pain. She summoned her brother, Ben, to rush her to the hospital.

At the ER, an attendant secured Rachel in a wheelchair. The ER was particularly busy, so they parked her in the hallway. Almost immediately, Rachel's cry of pain caught the attention of the ER staff. A nurse rushed to her side and exclaimed, "She's having a baby!" The place went into full-scale alert, and Elizabeth was born right there in the hallway before they could get Rachel to a room.

Marie was home alone when the call came, "This is the administrator at St. Vincent's Hospital. Your daughter has just had a baby. You need to come to the hospital immediately."

"I'm sorry," Marie said, "but this must be some sort of mistake. My daughter isn't pregnant." Marie began to tremble, realizing that something shocking was taking place out of the blue.

I was in my office at the church when Marie called me. The tone and nature of her voice told me that something drastic was in the works. Marie told me what she knew, and we couldn't make sense of anything as we drove to the hospital.

Why was it shocking? No one knew Rachel was pregnant! Not Rachel, not Marie, not me. Nobody but God. But that's another story.

We found Rachel in a recovery room bed on the maternity floor. All of us were speechless and crying. We did some quick processing to re-enter reality and soon I asked, "Where's the baby?" Can you guess Rachel's response?

"The needle-nato unit." I managed a smile and asked Rachel if she minded if I went.

Using my pastor and grandfather cards to gain admission. I went to Elizabeth's side. We were alone. In shock and with streaming tears, I said, "Hi Lizzie, this is Pop Pop. You're such a surprise! I'm so glad to meet you. This is the first thing in life I want you to hear," and I blubbered my way through the song, *Jesus Loves Me, This I Know*. I kissed her tiny cheek and left.

We saw that "needle-nato" unit for many days before Lizzie was able to go home. To this day we tease Rachel about the "needle-nato" unit.

But the "needle-nato" unit held another surprise for me. I was summoned to the same hospital to visit a family who didn't attend my church. The situation was critical – a premature baby weighing in at one pound, twelve ounces. His name was Joshua which means "Yahweh (God) is salvation." It's the Old Testament name for Jesus.

I requested to see a family member. Soon Beth Seip, the sister of Chris, the new mother, came through the door. She was a stranger to me. We chatted in the hall peering into the neo-natal unit window while

Beth told me all about the situation. Soon some family members joined us and, outside the door of the "needle-nato" unit, I prayed fervently with total strangers.

But here's the twist. Time passed and my son, Jason, fell in love with a lady named Beth. We began to connect the dots. It was the Beth that I met at the "needle-nato" unit. She's now my daughter-in-law. And the preemie Josh Edmiston? He's 5'10" and weighs in at 180 pounds.

Indeed, truth is stranger than fiction.

33

THE EMERGENCY

It was a February Sunday afternoon, after a heavy ministry week, when I called my mother. She lived on the other side of Pennsylvania near Philadelphia.

I'm known in my family for prank calls. The pressures of the week must have gotten to me for when my stepfather, Bob Landis, answered the phone, I immediately went into a spontaneous prank mode. In a female-sounding, somewhat desperate voice I said, "This is Nancy. I need help!"

I fully expected Bob to say something in response. But no. He slammed down the receiver and the conversation stopped in its tracks. Now what to do?

Nancy lived in the mobile home immediately next door to my mother and Bob. She was sickly, and several times Mom and Bob had taken her to the hospital.

Bob went on red alert like a paramedic. He was totally convinced it had been Nancy on the phone. It was cold, and snow lay on the ground. He was in his stocking feet. There was no time for a coat or shoes. Bob flew out the door.

I called back as quickly as I could. Mom answered the phone. She explained that Bob was already gone. There was nothing she could do.

Down their porch stairs Bob had bounded and up the porch stairs of Nancy's mobile home he went. No knock on the door. No doorbell. No anything. There wasn't time for that.

Bob thrust open the unlocked door. There sat Nancy in her living room. She was in total shock. Not because she was ill or in an emergency, but because she was simply relaxing in her recliner watching TV when in bursts this intruder.

It took Nancy a moment to recognize Bob, but soon she came to her senses. "Bob! What in the world are you doing?" Bob was just as shocked as Nancy. Words fled him as he scanned his brain trying to figure out what had just happened. It was apparent that there was no emergency.

Bob didn't know what to say. "Nancy, I'm so sorry! I got this call asking for immediate help and I thought it was you. It must have been a wrong number." He could barely conceal his sheepish countenance.

"Are you okay, Nancy?" asked Bob, still wanting to believe that she had called him for help. "Sure!" she said, "I'll be fine once my heart slows down." Another round of apologies flowed from Bob. And by then, Nancy had settled down. Pleasantries were exchanged, and Bob left.

He returned to his home perplexed – but not for long. Mom greeted Bob at the door with the story of what had *really* happened.

Bob is a great guy. He's easy-going, never causing anyone trouble. But I had to face the music. How would Bob take this prank that had gone to a whole other level?

I was quite tentative as I waited for his voice on the other end of the line. "Al, was that you who called?!"

He went on to tell me the whole story. He was gracious and, as he told the story, he began to laugh.

So did my mother. And so did I, almost uncontrollably. My wife didn't think it was that funny: "I told you that one of these days your pranks will get you into trouble."

I apologized. He accepted it as sincere even though my words were baptized in laughter. "Are you going to tell Nancy what happened?" I inquired. "No, I'm going to leave well enough alone," as he closed the case. To this day, Nancy doesn't have a clue about what really triggered Bob to the rescue.

For the rest of the day, every time I thought about my words, *This is Nancy. I need help!* and visualized what had transpired with Bob to the rescue, I shook with laughter.

I've often pondered this question since then, "Can I be truly sorry and keep laughing at the same time?" The answer is probably *No* because the prankster in me still rises up.

34

THE GARAGE DOOR OPENER

There are far too many remote controls in our home these days. It's almost like a plague. We've got six remotes just to run our TV, DVD player, and internet options.

Every so often, a stray remote shows up. We have no idea where it came from. The moment we'd throw it away, we'd find out where it belonged. So it keeps hanging around.

Such was the case with a stray garage door opener Marie came across one day.

"Where did this come from?" she asked. "It doesn't operate either of our garage doors."

I told her I had no clue. "But don't throw it away," I cautioned. "Let's put it in a cupboard and someday the mystery will be solved." Into storage it went.

Several years went by, and the time was nearing to finally dispose of the opener when I made a suggestion.

"Let me put it in my car. As I drive around town, for the fun of it, I'll see if it opens or closes any garage doors." Marie gave me a strange look as I assured her that it was more of a joke than anything else.

But I got curious. *I wonder if that remote would actually operate some random garage door in town. Sure wouldn't hurt to find out.* So on occasion, when I'd drive through a nearby neighborhood, I'd push the remote button. I wasn't surprised. No garage doors ever opened.

My son, Jared, had dated Wendy Braun some years before. In fact, at one point they had been engaged.

Once, a thought crossed Marie's mind and she said to me, "Could that remote belong to Wendy's parents?" We didn't think much more about it.

One summer night, after a series of stressful days, I announced to Marie, "I'm going to take a little spin. And while I'm at it, I'm going to see if I can open any garage doors. In fact, my target door is Wendy's parents' garage." It was after 11:00pm and I was almost certain it would be another dry run. I decided I'd toss the opener in the trash after this one last try.

Off I went into the night. I tried several doors as I drove around Millcreek. Nothing. It was exactly as I expected.

Well, I thought to myself, *I might as well try Wendy's house, and then I'll return home.*

I slowed down by their residence and pulled into the driveway. All the lights were out. Wendy's parents had retired for the night. *Let's give it a shot*, I thought, as I pushed the remote button.

I was stunned! The garage door responded. Up it ascended, and on went the light.

There was no way I was prepared for this. I froze. I didn't know what to do. The door was halfway up when I pushed the button again so the door would retreat. I prayed, *Oh God, please let Al and June be so sound asleep that they'll never hear it.*

My prayer went unanswered. Suddenly the house lights came on. The front door flew open. Out came Al and June Braun in robes, extreme surprise and confusion on their faces. The proceedings were a colossal mystery to them.

I bolted from the car towards them shouting, "It's me, Jared's dad!" Now they looked even more surprised. Once they realized that they weren't dreaming, they looked somewhat relieved.

Sheepishly I said, "You've got to hear this story. It will explain everything." They were more than ready to listen. As the story unfolded, the tension evaporated, and smiles settled on their faces. Strange as it first sounded, it all made sense. After a few moments, we all agreed it was very funny.

I apologized profusely for startling them with a late-night intrusion. My apologies were graciously received. I handed over the remote. They had no idea what had happened to it, but they were most grateful for its return.

I watched them retreat through the front door as I backed out of the driveway. I was embarrassed but at the same time struck with laughter. As I drove away, I reflected on how we agreed that maybe there was a better way to solve the mystery of the rogue garage door opener.

When I got home, Marie agreed as well and she shook her head with an "only you" smile.

35

DREAMS

Scientists say that everyone dreams at night. I'm particularly good at it. Almost every night I have vivid dreams. Unfortunately, most of them are scary. Psychologists call them "night terrors."

Some examples: tornadoes are approaching or a snake is slithering in my direction. I try to scream, but I'm paralyzed with fear. Or I stand behind a lectern on the stage. I know my topic, but I can't find my notes. Worse yet, I haven't prepared. I'm beyond embarrassed and totally self-conscious.

Or someone on my team has failed to complete an assignment. It wasn't a mistake. It was dereliction. I take them to task with little grace. Or I'm walking down a dark street when I'm ambushed by assailants. An actual blood-curdling, self-protecting scream escapes in real time while I act in self-defense.

Most of the time I'm awakened by the dream. I check reality and find I'm okay. I say to myself, *I've got to remember this dream!* But I don't.

I'm not the only one awakened. My poor wife's sleep has been interrupted countless times by the acting out of my dreams in real time. You see, these dreams are not just in my head. They manifest themselves in physical drama. While I remember virtually no dream by morning, Marie has a catalog of behaviors that accompany my dreams, like when I ratchet up and throw myself out of bed. For this reason, upper bunk beds are out for me at men's retreats.

Sometimes I draw back my leg and kick in self-defense. The same is true of flying fists. Marie has been the long-suffering recipient of bumps and bruises and yet remains most forgiving and gracious. As I dream, I laugh out loud. I cry. I whimper. I talk out loud, sometimes in complete sentences. And unbelievably, sometimes in sailor's language.

After all these years, my dear wife can see it coming. There's a stirring in my body, a twitching, a change in breathing cadence – all signals of an approaching dream storm.

She gently nudges me. She puts her hand on my shoulder. She caresses my back. She speaks softly to me. I respond and the dream dissipates or reroutes itself for a later time.

Not everyone is as seasoned in dealing with my dream episodes as Marie. My antics at night become unsettling and shocking experiences for the uninitiated. You see, my number one dream manifestation is a blood-curdling, deafening scream of horror. That still scares Marie and has shortened the life-span of several other unsuspecting souls.

These days when I have a roommate for the night, they get a crash course in dream warnings and self-defense. Take my son and daughter-in-law for instance. We shared a room on a trip to the United Kingdom. On the first night, as bedtime approached, I said, "Rachel, there's something you need to know. I have night terrors. I can't control them. I tend to scream. So just in case it happens, you need to know that everything's okay. No one's getting murdered."

She nodded her thanks, along with a look that expressed, *It probably won't happen.* But in the middle of the night, my prophecy came true. It wouldn't surprise me if I woke up half the hotel. Rachel, even with the warning before bedtime, was terrified. Of course, all I could do was apologize over waves of laughter. The next night, there was no scream.

Instead, they heard my operatic singing voice.

And then there was the guy who roomed with me in Israel. He was a pastor I had never met before. At bedtime the first night in Jerusalem I said, "Denny, I've been having these recurring snake dreams the last six months. They come at me, and I'm horrified. I scream something like you've never heard before. It'll scare you, but it's not a terrorist attack." Sure enough, about 3:00am, I scared Denny within an inch of his life.

One night, a bomb went off in my dream. There was an explosion of sound and light with shrapnel flying everywhere. There was nothing left to do but dive for cover. I found myself in a heap on the floor. The crown of my head was bleeding. I had hit the metal handle on the dresser next to the bed. Had I dived the other way, Marie would have been in the path of a direct hit.

Marie tells me that when I'm not diving or screaming or laughing or crying, I'm preaching or scolding or barking out orders of some kind. She remembers the dream until morning and tells me what I said and did. It's always good for a belly laugh.

Here's a sampling. Marie sensed something was coming. My body moved and I began to speak loudly, "My job is to make grown men cry! By the time I'm finished with you, you'll be miserable. But you'll be a disciplined group. Now strip down to your underwear!" I had no idea that during the night I had become a drill sergeant in the army.

I'd write my dreams down if I could remember them. There might be therapeutic interpretations that would help me by day. But let this serve as fair warning. If you're ever near me overnight, it could be a frightening experience. If you have a choice, you may want to sleep in another room.

36

THE MOTEL

A foursome friendship developed at Dallas Theological Seminary. We were in the same class, and for four years, Brian Christie, John Frye, Ray Clendenen, and I hung out together, thinking those days would never end. Then graduation came, and we went our separate ways. John and I stayed in touch sporadically, but I lost track of Ray and Brian.

The speed of life caught up with us. Suddenly, it was the 40th reunion of our seminary class. Through the wonder of Facebook, I was able to track down all three friends. I floated the idea of the four of us going to the reunion and spending the weekend together. Everyone jumped on board without hesitation. It was a go!

The volunteer in me offered to set up the motel arrangements. Looking over the seminary recommendations for a bargain, I started at the low end of the pricing bracket. I recognized a national motel chain, so I figured things ought to be decent. Besides, I was certain the seminary had done its homework. They'd never recommend a dive.

I made the phone call. "What do you have that will accommodate four guys?"

"We specialize in suites. There'll be plenty of space for all of you. It's a two-story unit," came the reply.

My next question was logical. "What's the price?"

"With your seminary discount, $79.00 per night. Plus taxes, $87.90," she replied. I was stunned.

"Is that per person?" I inquired.

"No," came the response. "That's the total for the room per night." With such a deal, I dismissed the nagging, negative intuition inside me.

I hit the jackpot, I thought to myself. *Let's see. A four-way split and that's only $22 bucks a night. The guys are going to love me.* I booked the suite. Yet it bugged me overnight as I thought, *Something doesn't sound quite right.*

The next morning, I called the seminary. The conversation went something like this, "I see you recommended such and such motel. How would you rate it?"

"Well, I don't know anything about it. But I'm sure we wouldn't have listed it if it weren't okay," said the seminary rep on the other end of the line.

I told him the price of the room and he said, "Such a deal. You'll be fine." I hung up the phone thinking that conversation wasn't very reassuring. But could my well-reputed seminary ever mislead their esteemed alumni?

Landing at the Dallas airport, I rented a car and began my journey to the motel. The area was getting somewhat industrial and rundown, but I began to think that my GPS might be malfunctioning. Sure enough, the motel was in this district.

Brian was the first to arrive. He's an accomplished attorney. He was sitting at the desk just inside the suite door using his laptop when I arrived. We hadn't seen each other in forty years. There was a hearty embrace and a barrage of back-and-forth catch-up conversation, as I listened once again to his winsome South African accent. I was oblivious to the accommodations.

127

Then came the question in colloquial language for an attorney, "Where in the world did you come up with a place like this?" I cringed as I scanned the surroundings. I told him the story of how I landed on this choice.

"We can move if you like," I offered.

"No," he said, "Ray won't arrive till after ten tonight. John will be staying with relatives."

When Ray arrived later that night, it was evident that no one was thrilled with my choice. The place was dirty, unkempt, unrepaired, and totally skin-crawling. I could go on.

As there weren't enough beds for everyone, in an act of penance, I volunteered to take the hide-a-bed. When I opened it, I got the creeps. It housed a stained, paper-thin mattress without a sheet, and just a blanket over unparalleled hills and valleys across the bed springs.

What was I to do? Complain to my friends and make them feel bad? Sit in a chair all night? Sleep standing up? I pretended that I was on the mission field in Africa and forced myself to crawl into bed. Refusing to spread out, I got into a tight little ball with my knees near my chin to take up as little real estate in that bed as possible. It was a terrible night. I can assure you, Brian and Ray fared a little better.

In the morning, it was my turn to shower. When I stepped into the tub, I looked down. The black on my feet from the dirt on the floor transferred to the tub, and streams of wet dirt flowed towards the drain. Appalled, right then and there I vowed, *We're outta here!*

I brought my decision to the attorney. He said, "I've already booked another motel – a *nice* motel. You're fired." And then Brian said these words I'll never forget. "I've not been in a place like this since Tina and I were poor." We all chuckled.

The upside? He paid the entire bill for the new motel and treated us all to an upscale dinner. I'm sure it was his way of extending me forgiveness and comforting Ray. Maybe John had stayed with his relatives for good reason.

We went on to have a great time at the reunion and at the upgraded motel, thanks to our "used-to-be-poor" lawyer friend who came to the rescue.

37

THE WHOPPER

No matter where you live, people like a white Christmas. The year 2017 was the deepest white Christmas I've ever experienced.

The National Weather Service said we could expect twelve to sixteen inches of snow starting late Christmas Eve. Big deal. We live in Erie, Pennsylvania. Snow accumulations of that magnitude are normal – nothing to worry about. It's not like we live in Virginia or Georgia where a few inches stop everything in its tracks.

It began as a normal Christmas Eve Day: last minute shopping, final food and house preparations, off to the Warner Theater in the afternoon for the community Christmas Eve service, and a slight breather after that. Evening came, and our Erie area family gathered at Grandpa Simmons's house for festive food and the traditional opening of gifts.

All of that with no snow on the ground.

I decided to recheck the weather forecast. This time, the winter storm warning said, *Up to 39 inches in some locations. The snow will begin after 9:00pm.* Thirty-nine inches? That would be a rare event indeed, even in Erie.

I went to Marie and said, "Do you want to hear something funny?

They're calling for 39 inches in some parts of our area. Never gonna happen." I'd have bet the farm.

As we left Grandpa's house that night, a light, lazy Christmas Eve snow had begun – so gentle and non-foreboding. I laughed again to myself, *Thirty-nine inches? And they pay these people.*

Marie and I settled in at home and, as is our custom, we stayed up until midnight to watch Christmas Eve slip into Christmas Day. I checked the snow again. It was still coming down with a little more intensity. Still unconcerned, we headed to bed.

Perhaps you remember the story about Daniel and the lion's den. King Darius consigned Daniel to his fate but had a terrible night of sleep. First thing in the morning, he went to see what was left of Daniel. He had the shock of his life – Daniel was in great shape thanks to the protective hand of God, and the lion's were as docile as pussycats.

I slept like a baby on Christmas Eve night. But like Darius, I rose early Christmas morning to peer out the window. I expected to see a few inches of snow. Instead, it was a winter wonderland. The snow was deep, falling fast and furious. I could barely see across the street.

Time to recheck the weather. Nothing had changed. *A winter storm warning and 39 inches in some areas.* I laughed again, still not believing.

Marie doesn't cook on Christmas Day now that the family has left the nest. Our big family celebration is always Christmas Eve. Several years before, I suggested to Marie, "With just a few of us on Christmas Day, don't cook anymore. Let's go to a restaurant for our Christmas dinner."

That suggestion was more than fine with her. When we checked our area restaurants, we discovered that every single restaurant was closed on Christmas Day. All except one. Chinese. It's become our yearly tradition.

Hungry for a good Christmas dinner, I ventured outside to assess the situation – not good. The snow was up to my knees. Maybe things would calm down in a few hours. But I alerted the few family members who were to join us for our Chinese dinner. "It's bad out there. Maybe dinner won't happen."

By noon, the decision was final. Snowed in. Make do at home. The snow continued.

Still, I was convinced the weatherman was wrong. It wouldn't be 39 inches. And it wasn't. By Tuesday morning when the snow finally stopped, we had 65 inches! I'd never seen anything like it. Our cars were buried. We had no idea when we'd be plowed out.

That afternoon, we began to dig out our cars. We gave it a Herculean effort, but it was too much. We'd have to wait for a plow – maybe Spring!

Suddenly Marie said, "I sure could go for a Whopper!" With my lingering Christmas spirit I said, "Why not?"

"You're not serious!" she exclaimed. "The roads are barely open and our cars are buried!"

"I know," I replied. "We'll walk there!" She was in disbelief!

As a first step, I called Burger King. "We're open," the clerk said. Only in Erie!

We bundled up like abominable snowmen and began our trek through the deep snow. Burger King was a mile-and-a-half away. The incredible beauty of nature was beyond description. But halfway there, I realized the danger of walking on a snow-narrowed major road with cars speeding past us.

We finally got to the restaurant to enjoy our Whoppers. But I decided that we wouldn't walk back – too exhausting and too dangerous.

I said nothing to Marie, but I began profiling the few intrepid customers who walked through the restaurant doors. For each, I tried to assess the likelihood of us getting a ride. *Not that man. Not that couple. Maybe that lady.*

Finally, in came the perfect couple. *That's the one!* I concluded almost instantly. I let them order and eat for a while. Then came the moment. I stood up and walked over to their table. Marie had that *what's Al doing?* look on her face.

"Hi! My name is Al. Merry Christmas. Do you mind if I ask you a few unusual questions and *then* tell you why?"

They looked at each other warily and said, "Go ahead."

"I live near McDowell High School. Do you live anywhere near there?"

They responded, "Yes," and I was overjoyed.

Next question, "Would you mind taking my wife and me home?" as I pointed towards Marie. I proceeded to explain the situation to the couple. They couldn't believe we had walked there. They smiled with mercy, and we had our ride.

On the way home, they marveled afresh at our adventure. During our conversation, we discovered that they were church-going folk and that we had many mutual friends. As we chatted, it felt to all of us that our "chance" meeting was definitely a God thing.

We'll always remember the Christmas of 2017 as "The Whopper Christmas" – a whopper of a snowstorm, Whoppers to eat, and two whopperly Good Samaritans who came to our rescue. And, the Christmas when the weather had the last laugh.

38

THE ENDLESS TRAIL

When they lived in California, sometimes Marie and I would vacation with our son, Jared, and his family. One day, four adults and three kids jumped into their Honda Pilot. It was a tight fit, but we made it thanks to some bungee cords holding our luggage on the roof rack.

We made our way northward for the three-and-a-half-hour ride to Sequoia National Park. We had reservations in a secluded ranch house high upon a lonely mountain. The three-and-a-half-hour ride stretched into nearly five. We got lost on back roads and our GPS wasn't all that cooperative. It was a preview of what was to come.

After two days of sightseeing in the park, we decided to walk the popular riverside trail to the mighty Tokopah Falls. We saw a steady stream of people returning from their hike there.

We were about to begin when I asked one of the returnees, "About how far is it to the Falls?" "Oh, about one and a half miles," he replied. With all the walking we had done the past few days, not a problem.

Well, maybe one. Our smallest grandson, Micah, was two, and he needed a stroller. We peered down the trail. A nice wide, dirt path lay before us. It looked like it narrowed in the distance. But maybe the narrowing was only the *perspective* of distance. We started out.

It was actual, not perspective. The path *did* narrow. And with the narrowing came a major complication. The trail was littered with rocks and boulders. Not only that, the trail inclined upward. There was a series of slippery and foreboding rocky steps ahead. I spoke to Jared, "I don't think this is gonna work. Micah is too heavy to carry, and we have his stroller to deal with. Maybe we should turn around."

Jared was always the kind of person up for a challenge. Nothing could deter him. So it wasn't much of a surprise when my suggestion fell on deaf ears.

As the trail became narrower and rockier, people that passed us on their return trip volunteered, "You're not gonna make it. You'll never get a stroller much further." They were right. But with Jared, Plan B was not to return. It was to forge ahead. He carried Micah. I carried the stroller. We walked and stumbled forward. People kept telling us, "You'd better turn around. It's going to get worse."

Jared is a psychologist. We've talked about how often we're in the counseling room and tell people what's ahead. If they keep going in the same direction, it won't be good. We both agreed how amazing it is that people keep going.

I played that card, "Jared, the people we're passing have *been* to the Falls. They know what's ahead. Everyone's telling us to turn around." His response? "Perseverance pays off." He wouldn't be dissuaded. Marie heard his answer and said to me, "You should know by now that telling Jared he can't do something is like saying sick-um to a dog." It was forward toward the Falls.

It seemed like we must have walked at *least* a mile when I began to ask returning passers-by, "How much further to the Falls?" Their constant response, "About half a mile." We'd walk some more, until I was sure we had walked another half-mile. But I couldn't see or hear the Falls. So I asked some more returning hikers, "How far to the Falls?" Back

135

came the response, "Oh, about half a mile." *What?!*

We proceeded forward. The path gave way to a rocky and steep slope. Micah weighed a ton by now. And the stroller? I was ready to hide it and pick it up on the way back. We continued walking what seemed like another mile. I asked another hiker, "How far?" "Oh, about half a mile," came the reply. I couldn't believe it!

The same kind of thing happened in the 1943 movie "Girl Crazy" starring Mickey Rooney (Danny) and Judy Garland. Danny's father shipped him off to all-male Cody College out West. Upon disembarking at Cody Village, he discovered there were no taxis. He was told he must walk eight miles to the college. Miles later he sees a road sign – "Cody College, 8 miles." He walked quite a distance more when he came to another sign – "Cody College, 8 miles." He kept walking until he finally reached a third sign – "Cody College, 8 miles."

We kept walking what seemed to be another half-mile when I asked someone again, "How far?" You guessed it, "Oh, about half a mile." I began to think the trail was endless and these people had conspired to come up with this standard answer, *Oh, about half a mile.* By now, it was getting funny. No matter how far we walked, back came the same answer. There was nothing factual about this "half a mile" business.

We finally heard the Falls. And then we saw a majestic sight – the cascading of water from a cliff high above, emptying into a basin of rainbow-colored mist. Jared's perseverance had paid off. It made me think of a line from that old Southern Baptist preacher, Vance Havner, when climbing to the top of a challenging mountain, "The view was worth the distance."

Soon we were on our way back. On occasion, somebody would ask me, "About how far to the Falls?" You can guess my answer. "Oh, about half a mile."

39

THE ROOSTER

I s there another animal besides a cat that has nine lives? The answer? *Yes! My brother-in-law's rooster.*

Glenn lives in a rural setting some 35 miles northwest of Philadelphia. His house overlooks a steep slope. A lazy, little stream separates the slope from the gentle valley below. There's a bridge that crosses the stream to two chicken houses.

Glenn has raised brown-egg laying hens for over 40 years. There are no zoning restrictions about raising animals there. On our visits, we hear the roosters crowing in the morning.

These chickens have personalities all their own. Glenn knows them, and they know him. They're not so sure about us when we approach them. But Glenn is their hero. They love what he feeds them.

But the ruling rooster, well, he was the jealous type. He oversaw his harem, and no one could befriend him, not even Glenn.

Every time we'd visit, we'd inquire about the rooster and his ongoing antics. Mind you, Glenn is a grown man. He's not tall, and he's of slender build. But next to that rooster, David and Goliath wouldn't be a fair comparison. Glenn is a monster beside that feathery little beast.

And beast is the right word. In fact, it may be too mild a term. With no recognition that Glenn was many times larger than he, that rooster would take him on as an equal.

Here's how it played out. Glenn would go down to feed the brood. The rooster would perk up. Then it would go diversionary. It would fake-peck at seed on the ground pretending not to see Glenn. But he was watching Glenn's every move, just waiting for the opportune time to attack.

As soon as Glenn would turn his back the slightest, the rooster would mount a full-fledged attack. He'd come at breakneck speed, feathers unfurled, with talons flashing. To the rooster, it was do or die. It was for Glenn, too. He had to protect himself or that rooster was liable to kill him.

Over the years, Glenn learned to protect himself. He kept a long, wooden stick to fight off that bird. The rooster had a high pain threshold. He cared not if he took a beating. His aim was to get rid of Glenn at all costs.

You'd think a rooster would have half a brain. If he'd always get the tarnation beaten out of him on the attack, call a truce. Let Glenn in the chicken house without a fight. Not a chance.

And Glenn? How much grace do you extend to a mad little monster? A lot, because Glenn let that bird live long after most people would have had him for Sunday dinner.

On each visit, I'd inquire, "Do you still have that rooster?" Glenn would reply, "Yes." I'd say, "Surely, by now he's tamed down." "Nope," would come the amazing retort, and I'd ask Glenn to tell me the latest stories.

The rooster finally met its match. It was another rooster that was introduced into the brood. The beast and the new rooster didn't hit it off too well. One day, when no one was present, the roosters had it out. The new rooster won. When Glenn came to the chicken house, the meanest rooster in the world lay near death. The next stop would be rooster heaven. He lay there lifeless.

Glenn understands the food chain in the country. There are foxes and coyotes and minks who try to raid the chicken houses. And sometimes they've been tragically successful. On this occasion, Glenn made it easy for them. He took the rooster and laid it by the stream. It would be somebody's supper.

The next morning, the bird was gone. Glenn thought the food chain had prevailed. Instead, it was the walking dead. Incredibly, that rooster had resurrected himself and was hanging out by the chicken house. Just as incredible, Glenn decided to give "Lazarus" another chance!

That bird healed in seven days to the point you'd never know it had been gravely injured. The big questions were – would there be a behavioral change in the rooster? And, would there be a behavioral change in Glenn?

The answer on both fronts was – no. The rooster would go through the same antics just waiting for the opportune moment to strike. And Glenn would prepare to defend his life as always.

On a recent visit, I asked, "So, Glenn, do you still have that rooster?" I was shocked when he said, "No, I sold it at auction up the line. I now have another rooster and a whole new brood of laying hens. And *this* rooster is behaving himself."

I had to wonder if the man who bought the beast got the shock of his life. Or some night, would Glenn have to do battle again with a nine-lives rooster who found his way home.

40

TOILET TALES

Tradition can be defined as a special custom and practice of a family or group over a long period of time. *Insanity* has been defined as doing the same thing over and over again and expecting different results. Sometimes the difference between tradition and insanity can be blurred.

My sister and her husband, Joyce and Glenn Halteman, have lived in the same house for over 50 years. It's a quaint house in the country near where they grew up. Marie and I have made countless trips to their house. They are the consummate hosts. But I have to wonder about their guest bathroom.

Is what happens there tradition or insanity? You see, the toilet keeps clogging, and only for me.

At first, I thought it was a one-time occurrence. I sheepishly exited the bathroom to find Glenn. "Uh, Glenn. Might you have a plunger anywhere?" He bounded down the basement stairs and soon reappeared with the tool. Of course, he vanished. But with a little bit of work, I had the problem solved.

On another trip, another clog. *It happened again, but it's probably a fluke,* I mused. "Oh Glenn! Where's that plunger?"

Not to be denied, it happened *again* on a subsequent trip. Glenn appeared with the plunger. But this time, he looked a little strangely at me like *you're pushing the envelope here. Certainly, it can't have happened again!*

It did - on another trip. This time I found my sister and said in a whisper, "Might you know where the plunger is?" Joyce retorted, "You've got to be kidding!" She thought I was joking. But no, I was serious as I added, "I'll take care of it. You don't need to tell Glenn."

I started to dread that toilet! There was hardly a trip in which it didn't happen. I knew Joyce and Glenn were weary of my plunger requests. But once clogged, I knew staring at it wouldn't solve the problem. After a while, they began to lovingly roll their eyes. That's when I tried to make sure Glenn was nowhere in sight when I made my reluctant plunger requests.

We had several trips where nothing happened. I was counting my blessings. I thought, *The toilet is finally okay. It's good to go. The future is bright.* Plunging was becoming an amusing memory.

And then it happened again. Big time. Joyce smuggled the plunger to me. I worked and worked. Sweat beads ran down my brow. I'd flush and the water would flirt with overflowing the top of the bowl. Nothing I did solved the problem. That's when Joyce told me her story. By the way, they own a cleaning service. In her own words:

One Friday, I was cleaning a house. I needed to use their bathroom. I'm very private about using someone's bathroom if they're home, so typically I would just "hold it in." Thankfully, they had taken their two dogs to the vet, and I was to lock up when I left. So I used the toilet hoping it wouldn't clog. It did.

The plunger was useless; it kept turning inside out. The water reached the brim, so I got a cup from the kitchen and found a bucket. I'd flush and dip, taking several trips to the flower bed. I finally used the toilet bowl brush, trying to push the clog through. It broke in the neck of the toilet and wouldn't budge.

I went to the kitchen to get a fork. Being careful not to scratch the toilet, I tried to pry the brush loose, but to no avail. I was beyond upset. I cleaned the cup, fork, and bucket in Clorox and hot soapy water and finished the cleaning job. I wrote them a brief note, telling them that I was sorry, and that I'd pay the plumbing bill.

That weekend, we went to the Pocono Mountains with friends. As we left for our trip, I was still upset. But halfway up to the mountains, I started to giggle as I told our friends about my toilet episode. The next morning when I got up, there was a plunger outside my door.

When I called my clients on Monday, they told me the plumber had to remove the toilet and take it out on the sidewalk to work on it. And then they told me that I didn't ever have to come back to clean. They never sent me a bill.

As Joyce finished her story, Glenn arrived at my clog scene, shaking his head about the brother-sister conversation. And then he did what only a true brother-in-law would do. He took that plunger and maneuvered it like a speeding piston, unable to contain the splash. It finally unclogged, and he saved the day. I was afraid he'd say, *Don't ever come back.*

I finally learned how to use that testy toilet. But every so often, I sneak into the kitchen to find Joyce and say in a whisper, "Can you get me the plunger?" She takes the bait in disbelief until I say, "Just kidding."

These days, Joyce puts a little motion-activated figurine on the top of the toilet when we visit. It says things like, "Well, come on in. I've saved you the best seat in the house." And "Come on in. Shut the door. Have a seat, rest your feet, and sit here on the throne." And "Well, hello. It's always good to see one of my regulars." And "What brings you here? On second thought, I really don't want to know."

That crazy figurine is now a welcome tradition just in case the insanity should return.

II

Humorous Stories From My Ministry

41

THE STENCH

Marie and I were newlyweds and volunteer youth group leaders at Kildare Avenue Baptist Church, a small church on the northwest side of Chicago.

We were also custodians of the church. Part of the job included getting the church ready for Sunday morning services in the dead of winter and mopping up water in the basement from every torrential rain. For that, we got free rent in the second-floor apartment next to the church. The pastor and his family lived below.

Fall came and with it, the wide swings in temperature that occur regularly in the Chicago area.

It was a perfect time for a youth extravaganza. We created a fun and scary Halloween experience in one of the many northern forest preserves in the Chicagoland area. The turnout was great and the event was a crowd-pleaser. Marie and I had a deep sense of satisfaction. We loved those kids.

It was a chilly night for the outing, so nothing but some authentic hot chocolate with whipped cream would do. Borrowing a large table-top, metal thermos, we filled it with the real deal – not water and a powdered mix but real milk hot chocolate. It was a homerun with the youth.

After the event, we wanted to leave the forest preserve better than we found it so we quickly gathered up all the props for games, the trash, and the leftover food and drink. When we grabbed the large metal thermos, we were surprised to feel some leftover hot chocolate in it.

Back at our apartment, we took care of everything from the outing immediately except for one thing – the thermos. For some reason, I sat the thermos on our second-floor porch just outside our rarely used back door. Why I let it sit there for eight days I can't tell you. But there were always other things to do. And, I guess - out of sight, out of mind.

Finally, Marie suggested, "Don't you think you'd better deal with that hot chocolate thermos and return it to its owner?" Yes, she had delegated that responsibility to me. As a newlywed, I didn't object.

Do you recall that I said there were great temperature swings in Chicago in the Fall? It went repeatedly from the upper 40s to the lower 80s over the eight days the thermos sat there.

Champ was the friendliest, little Schnauzer. He lived with the pastor's family below. Every time he heard us on the porch above, Champ would bound up the stairs and nestle against us, stubby tail vibrating almost as fast as hummingbird wings.

I was out on the porch, finally ready to deal with the thermos. Champ heard me and bounded up the stairs. Marie joined us. I petted Champ and then I stooped to open the thermos. I had no clue as to the power and smell of fermented, spoiled milk. But I was about to find out.

The lid was difficult to turn but once there was a small breach in the seal, the pressure that escaped almost blew the top off. With the escaping air, there also came an all-encompassing, overwhelming, indescribable stench. I finished removing the lid and fell backwards away from the thermos.

Not Champ. He stuck his nose into the mouth of the thermos. Suddenly we heard a bloodcurdling shriek from Champ like he'd been shot. His head flew back and, putting his little tail between his legs, he ran like greased lightning down the stairs. We heard his deafening howl all the way to the refuge of his owner's apartment door below.

Poor Champ! We feared we may have traumatized him beyond repair and damaged our relationship. It took him a whole week, but finally, slowly, and cautiously, he ventured up the stairs.

On the top stair, he scouted out the porch. The thermos was gone, so he ran to us and nestled up to us once again.

From that time until the snow flew, every time Champ heard us on the porch above, he sped up those stairs for a friendly visit. All was forgiven.

Perhaps there are a couple lessons here from Champ. Don't procrastinate. And hold no grudges.

42

THE KITCHEN FIGHT

Heat in the kitchen is fundamental to its proper functioning. But sometimes there's another kind of heat in the kitchen – the heat of an argument. That kind of heat can happen in the kitchens of homes, restaurants, and even churches.

In my first ministry in the Chicago area, the kitchen was used all the time. We had two of the best cooks any church could have – Elsie Swanson and Britt Nelson. We couldn't get enough of their cooking.

But on Sunday mornings, the kitchen was quiet.

Adjacent to the gym, where coffee, juice, and rolls were served on Sunday mornings, the doors to the kitchen were always open. Sometimes people would step in for a little privacy or just to get a drink of water.

That's exactly what I was doing – getting a drink of water at the sink – when I witnessed the following exchange.

Eudora and her husband, Clarence, were pillars of the church. You couldn't go to church and not see them. They were very sociable, the kind of couple that makes a church friendly. Eudora was also quite outspoken, but no one ever took offense.

Chris was newer to the church, as well as to the faith. She was connecting well, and she and her family had found a comfortable church home. She could also be outspoken.

Chris had a habit which many church people look down on – smoking. She wanted to quit but she wasn't quite there yet. She felt accepted at church, even though many knew that she struggled with her addiction.

On this particular Sunday, both women wandered into the kitchen at about the same time. Eudora saw her chance to have a one-on-one conversation with Chris. They exchanged pleasantries, and I was about to leave when the conversation got interesting. I lingered. Both ladies knew I was there.

"So how long have you been a Christian?" Eudora asked.

"A couple years," was the reply.

"Don't you think it's time to quit smoking?"

The sabers began to rattle. I saw some fire ignite in Chris's eyes. She felt attacked and began to raise her defenses.

"I know I should, and I'm trying to work on it." There was a pause. Some heat was coming. "I don't really think my smoking is any of your business," retorted Chris.

Not to be deterred, Eudora said again, "You need to quit smoking. When do you plan to stop?"

I could feel the heat rising even higher on Chris's side and I wondered with great curiosity what she would say next. Her reply took me by surprise. It was a classic.

"You're fat and you've been a Christian for a long time. When are *you* going to lose weight?"

Eudora had met her match, but she wasn't going to let Chris distract her that easily. So she repeated herself, "You need to quit smoking. When do you plan to quit?"

I could see that this new Christian could handle herself against a seasoned veteran. With a final verbal jab, she shut Eudora down for good.

"When you lose weight, I'll quit smoking."

I felt like a referee in the ring with two boxers. Throughout the conversation, I kept wondering if I should intervene. But seeing no "blood," I decided to let them duke it out.

That was it. Chris had the last word and they parted company. I was ready to do some relational mopping up after the service, if need be, but it wasn't necessary. Two outspoken people had sparred. They took their lumps and continued like nothing had happened.

I've often wished that more church people would fight like this: say your piece, let the other person say theirs, don't become offended, then walk away still friends.

It's those "behind your back" conversations that do the most damage, not the heat in the kitchen.

43

THE TAP DANCER

While serving as a youth pastor in the Chicago area, we provided a wide range of ministries and activities for our students. In addition to our worship services, we offered a dynamic Sunday School class and weekly in-home youth group meetings on Sunday nights. From there, we bolstered our programs with retreats, trips, drama presentations, invitational events, and various other ministries outside our church. Sometimes this led to interesting experiences.

One Sunday afternoon, our small traveling singing and drama youth team was ministering in an African-American church on the near north side of Chicago. We had partnered with the church before, so we had familiarity with each other.

Their church service was divided into the worship time, the offering, and preaching. Our youth team ministered during the first segment.

When it was time for the offering, the pastor exhorted his congregation to be generous and cheerful in their giving. He took a little extra time with his remarks, which took the form of a mini-sermon. At his signal, the ushers came forward. The electronic organ reverberated with spectacular improvisations on a gospel song.

Soon the ushers brought the offering to the front of the church and placed it carefully on the communion table in front of the pastor. They surrounded the table and the counting began.

It was intriguing. I'd been in churches from Philadelphia to Chicago, from Dallas to Los Angeles. This was the first count-the-money-on-the-spot offering I had ever seen. I wondered why the counting of the money didn't happen in another room or sometime after the service. I was soon to find out.

"Brothers and sisters," began the pastor. "We didn't collect enough money in the offering today." He proceeded to give another little offering pep talk. The organ once again swelled. The ushers took another offering and brought the plates to the front. The counting recommenced, all while the congregation sang with gusto.

"Praise God!" exclaimed the pastor after he got the results. "We've had a fine offering. Let's continue our service."

Almost immediately, an older gentleman ascended the platform. We had no printed order of service but we expected the sermon to be next. I later learned that this was totally impromptu.

"Before our pastor brings the message, I'm the special music. I'm going to sing you a song. But before I do, I'm going to give you my testimony." He began to tell his story.

"Before I met the Lord, I used to live my life in the world. I used to go to bars and places where I could drink and do what I was really good at – tap dancing. I mean, I was really good. No one could tap dance like me."

"Then when I got saved, I left all the things of the world behind, including my tap dancing. I never tap-danced again. Instead, the Lord gave me a voice. God took away my tap dancing and put singing in its place. And now I sing as good as I used to tap dance."

I can't deny it. This piqued my interest. With a build-up like that, I couldn't wait to hear his solo.

When he began to sing, Marie and I glanced at each other with a look that only married people know how to interpret. There was no denying that he put his whole heart and soul into his singing. But it was the joyful noise we read about in the Psalms – devoid of any skill. The crowd cheered him on. He thought he had hit a home run. The best we could do was to give him an "A" for effort.

On the way home, I turned to Marie and said, "If his singing was as good as his tap dancing, I sure wish I could have seen him tap dance!" We chuckled.

Later in my ministry, there were times we ran behind in our church budget. The offerings weren't always good. But if there were ever times I was tempted to get before the people, count the money, and say, "We're going to pass the plates again," I'd remember the tap dancer turned soloist and smile and we'd move on in the service.

44

THE BAPTISM

As a kid, I loved to swim. Get me by a farm pond or by the community pool and I was like a fish in water. But in my adult years, water became less appealing. Getting into a pool became an undesirable and rare thing.

This aversion for water started in my early twenties. I chalk it up to a change in life stage. It's like some foods. You loved them as a kid but they're not your favorites as an adult.

In my fourth year of seminary, we had a course on practical pastoral ministry. We were schooled in things like weddings, funerals, the ordinances, counseling, organization, and administration.

Seminary life is busy. I decided that I'd cruise a little in this course. I'd do what was necessary to get by, but I wouldn't give it my usual stellar effort. After all, I wasn't yet in the ministry.

I thought, *Couldn't I learn most of these things by doing once I graduated? It would be more relevant then. Every guy needs a class or two in which to coast.*

One day in class we came to the subject of the ordinances. The professor, Dr. Evans, talked about communion and the various ways it's done in different traditions. I knew what I was raised with and assumed it would be my method when I got into ministry. Hence, I didn't pay a lot of attention.

And then he said, "Our next class will be held at the YMCA pool in downtown Dallas. We're going to talk about baptism. I'll show you several techniques and then you'll all practice baptizing each other."

I thought to myself, *How relevant can this be? Doing baptism is a long way off in ministry. And I don't want to get in the pool. I'll do just fine once I get into ministry.*

I cut that class and never thought twice.

Graduation finally came and that June, Marie and I arrived at Skokie Valley Baptist Church in Wilmette, Illinois, our first ministry. The church sanctuary was an attractive A-frame type structure out of the 1960s accompanied by some education space and a medium-sized gym. The attendance was around 250.

As youth pastor, I had a lot of ministries going. Amazingly, I had little need to refer back to that practical ministry class at seminary. All was running smoothly.

Before long, the Senior Pastor resigned. An interim pastor, Lloyd Dahlquist, came on board and many of the ministerial duties fell to him.

All except one. Baptism.

The baptistery was elevated behind the choir loft in the center of the front wall of the sanctuary. Ladies entered the pool from the right and men from the left. Several people in the church inquired about baptism. As a young pastor, I was excited to oblige them.

We went through a preparatory class. All the arrangements were made. The date was set, and we were in for an exciting Sunday morning baptism. I never gave a thought to the mechanics of baptism nor to any challenges the baptismal candidates might present.

I entered the baptismal waters reluctantly because I don't enjoy the sensation of getting wet. But my adrenaline was pumping, and I was all set to baptize for my first time ever. I was beyond excited.

A deacon sent the first candidate in from the left. It was Clarence Polansky. That's when I panicked inside. Clarence was about 5'7" and weighed in at 275 pounds. Suddenly I thought, *How am I going to do this?* My next thought was, *How stupid of me not to take that baptism class in the YMCA pool!*

I stood facing the congregation. Clarence stood at a right angle to me. I asked him a few questions about his faith and his desire to be baptized so all could hear. I was hoping I could drag out the interview. But time pressed upon me, and I could delay no longer.

I grabbed the back of Clarence's robe between his shoulders with my right hand and put pressure on his chest with my left. I was going to pull and push to get him completely under. I couldn't think of any other way.

About halfway down, Clarence slipped out of my grip. His body started to free fall and instead of going down backwards, he rotated to his side until his backside faced the audience. This disturbance in the water created a mini tidal wave. Water went sailing over the top of the pool into the choir loft. Fortunately, the choir had already sung and vacated the area.

Now my task was to retrieve Clarence. It wouldn't be easy. I grabbed his robe and slippery arms and pulled him upwards. There was some buoyancy from the water, and he finally resurfaced.

He had a huge grin on his face and, as he spoke to me, the microphone picked up his words: "Did my feet break water?" He soon found his feet and looked over the pool to the moderately drenched choir loft. The whole church was next to uncontrollable with laughter.

I'll never forget Clarence and my first baptism and how I wished I had practiced with the guys in seminary. And Clarence? He couldn't have cared less about my problem and what happened. For him, it was a meaningful experience with a humorous "twist" that he'd always remember with fondness.

45

KILLING ENGLISH

Several professions – like lawyers, advertisers, salespeople, and pastors – make their living by using words. Unfortunately, I had some unique word challenges as I entered the field of preaching – including the influence of the Pennsylvania Dutch language. I couldn't speak it, but growing up in the heart of Pennsylvania Dutch country some thirty miles north of Philadelphia, it definitely left its imprint on me.

It started with my father. The influence of Pennsylvania Dutch made its greatest impact on his reversing of the letters "v" and "w." So when he liked something, it was "wery good." Or when he sang this old hymn, it was "Wictory in Jesus." And if he liked the soloist, she had a good "woice."

There was another swapping of letters – the "th" for the "f." Dad went to the "baffroom." He used a "toofpick" after a meal. And if he carried two things at the same time, he was carrying "bofe" of them.

Beyond this grand reversal of alphabet letters, my father managed a general crucifixion of the English language in general. You put the plug into a "receptible." That funny trio of comedians were "The Three Scrooges." A celebrative party was a "shindoo." The notorious Chicago gangster of the 1930s was "Al Capoon." He always wanted to go to that paradise 50th state, "Hawoya," but never got there. When his hands were cold, he wore "glubs." When he took our family to Washington, D.C. in 1963 to see President Kennedy's funeral procession, he was looking for the "captible." And he was so grateful for our missionary friends in "Ethiothia."

While I was able to get past my father's English missteps, I wasn't as fortunate with the Pennsylvania Dutch influence. They tend to invert words and phrases in sentences. They throw Mama down the stairs her shoes. And they throw the cow over the fence some hay. I, too, suffer from an "inversion of words" syndrome.

The Pennsylvania Dutch also have a whole esoteric vocabulary that you must unlearn. When something is empty, it's "all." When the wind messes up your hair, it's "strubley." When you clean up after a meal, you "red the table." When you have a whimpering cry, you're "brutzing." When you want someone to come to your house after lunch you say, "Come over this after." When it's time to go to bed, you "outen the lights."

Add to this the common mispronunciations by people in general to which I am not immune. Words like "prostrate" for "prostate," "nucular" for "nuclear," "realator" for "realtor," "sherbert" for "sherbet," "jewlery" for "jewelry," "calvary" for "cavalry," "physical" for "fiscal," and "mute" for "moot."

And then there was my father-in-law, John Simmons, who hailed from Peoria, Illinois. It turns out that his English wasn't much better than my dad's. For instance, when my wife was having lunch with him one day, he complained, "The doctor tells me that I have 'immaculate' degeneration." And when he did his taxes, the tax man told him that he could "deteriorate" some of his capital improvements. And when he had back pain, he wanted to visit the "choirpacter."

Try as I might, I've never been able to fully rise above these influences.

For instance, I was in Chicago with some of my staff attending a conference. At the end of the day, we went out for dinner. We were having a jolly time around the table when the waitress asked if anyone wanted drinks. Everyone ordered soft drinks. But I thought I'd get a rise out of them. When it was my turn to order I said with authority, "I'll have a *piñata* colada." The table exploded with laughter. I thought it was because they thought their Senior Pastor was going to order an alcoholic drink.

I thought I'd be cool when I fake-ordered my drink. I had no clue I had mispronounced it. It should have been "*piña* colada." They took delight in correcting me in the midst of their almost uncontrollable laughter. I managed to order a Pepsi. But I heard about *piñata* coladas for months afterwards.

These mispronunciations have followed me into the pulpit. When my son Jared was in high school and quite the wordsmith, he became a self-appointed critic of my sermon mistakes. When they'd happen, he'd meet me at the lobby door and thoroughly enjoy rehearsing my miscues. I knew it was lots of fun for him to catch his father in a blunder, and I rather enjoyed how much he reveled in catching me in them.

In the spirit of full disclosure, part of the problem stemmed from the fact that Jared and I would frequently engage in spoonerisms at home. A spoonerism transposes the initial sounds or letters of two or more words for humorous effect, like "slopping your drippers." Unfortunately, spoonerisms would follow me into the pulpit as well. One of my classics was when I talked about the danger lurking in every "crook and nanny."

There have been many sermon miscues in my career and there will be many more. As Jesus said the poor will always be with us, so it is with mispronunciations. They'll always be with me.

Time moves on, and Jared moved away. I sure do miss him at the lobby door.

46

WEDDING BLUNDERS

During my ministerial career, I've performed more than 400 weddings. With that many weddings, a pastor is sure to accumulate a collection of funny stories. I've certainly had a few memorable mishaps of my own. But if I were keeping score, the mishaps would be far more in the wedding party's column than in mine.

Fortunately, I've never had a major screw-up. Most of the time, it's a mispronounced word or forgetting something in the order of service. Usually, the only people that notice are my wife and me. But sometimes I haven't been so lucky.

I was doing an outdoor wedding in a park. Everything was going along well, including the the groom skateboarding down the aisle to the pleasant, but stunned, surprise of the bride.

But I stumbled in the vows.

"Repeat after me. I, Randy, take you, Beth, to be my wedded wife. And I do promise and covenant..." And we finished his vows.

Now it was the bride's turn.

"Repeat after me. I, Beth, take you, Randy." I momentarily left my notes and smiled affectionately at them and continued, "to be my wedded *wife*." I had lost my place. Beth snapped to attention and looked a brief, sugar-coated dagger at me. She didn't know if I was serious or kidding. I was serious but it was a mistake, and my beet-red blush gave me away. The crowd howled as I fought to regain my focus for the rest of the wedding.

* * *

The wedding kiss is always a highlight in a wedding. I coach the couple to make it a crowd-pleaser. At the appointed time, I love to give the couple their signal to kiss. But what came out of my mouth at one wedding took everyone by surprise, including me. I made the formal declaration pronouncing them husband and wife and followed it with this directive, "Eric, you may now *cuss* your bride." How do you recover from that?

* * *

At another wedding, everything had gone incredibly well. Not one mistake! With a mix of relief and confidence, I closed my notebook and began to say my final line, "It's my pleasure to present to you for the first time, Mr. and Mrs. ...." And then I went completely blank. I couldn't recall their names even though I knew them well. Incredibly, I had to whisper to them, "What's your name?" The couple looked a little stunned and the church erupted in laughter. It was a truly bad time to draw a blank!

* * *

My most memorable blunder was in my rookie year of ministry. I was asked to do a wedding in Chicago in an unfamiliar church. I took extra care to study my new environment so I could take this couple as flawlessly as possible through their special day.

The day arrived. A soloist was part of the prelude. Then the organ took over. The groom, groomsmen, and I took our place on the platform. The pretty bridal attendants made their way one-by-one down the aisle to their appointed spots.

The organ changed gears and signaled the entrance of the bride. Everyone stood when the bride's mother arose. The resplendent bride was soon by her groom.

It was time to begin. I addressed the standing crowd, "Dearly beloved." Then I began my introductory remarks and prayed the invocation. Afterwards, I enjoined the congregation, "You may be seated."

As I looked over the people, I noticed a man seemingly standing about halfway back on my right-hand side. I repeated, being careful not to look in his direction, "You may be seated." Nothing changed. I'm thinking, *Why doesn't that guy sit down!?* I didn't want to draw any more attention to the situation, so I continued through the entire ceremony.

Everyone stood at the end of the wedding and began to file out. Again, something caught my attention. It was that man. Now it looked like he was standing on the pew. I moved in his direction to spy out the situation.

To my surprise, his feet were on the floor. He was the tallest man I had ever seen, and he was wearing the largest pair of shoes I had ever seen. It finally dawned on me. He'd been sitting all along. But he was so tall that when sitting, he looked like he was standing.

Eventually, I spoke with the bride and groom. The bride said, "You must have met my uncle by now. He's the tallest man in the world."

His name was Don Koehler and he stood 8'2" tall. I checked the Guinness Book of World Records and there he was.

At every wedding since then, I only ask once for the people to be seated. And I realize anew that doing an absolutely perfect wedding is as scarce as a perfect game for a baseball pitcher.

47

THE SAXOPHONE

Weddings are a staple in pastoral ministry, and I don't marry lightly. Since marriage is a wonderful, yet difficult relationship, premarital counseling has always been a requirement for my weddings. It's frank, intense, candid, and preparatory. I want to do all I can to get couples off on the right foot.

Even though premarital counseling is valuable, I've often discovered that couples aren't tuned into the realities of which we speak. Somehow, they don't think they're going to have difficulties and challenges. The idealism they have towards each other overshadows the human natures they actually possess.

Premarital counseling is like learning to fly an airplane in the hangar. You're not up in the air in actual conditions. It's not until couples are married that what we talk about will make total sense to them. If I could, I'd cover the minimum bases before a couple gets married and then take them through a counseling program during their first year of marriage. I bet it would be more effective.

Sometimes the couples are 20 or 21 years old. As they sit across the counseling table from me, they look so young, and I wonder if they know what they're doing. Never mind that Marie was 19 and I was

21. But when older couples come to me, we're likely dealing with more maturity. It tends to feel better to me.

So in comes Jena, 28, and David, 31. They both had dating experience but it never went anywhere, until they found each other. They were mental health professionals, and I felt like they'd really "get" what we'd be talking about. But I wasn't going to take any shortcuts.

We arranged the schedule for four sessions. The first session would be the basic information about the wedding. The second session would be a discussion about the results of their temperament analysis. The third session would deal with the many practical matters of marriage. In the final session, we'd put the wedding together.

We came to the final session. We laid out all the possible elements of the ceremony, putting it together in a preliminary order. Then we changed some things, added some things, and put some things on hold. We completed a rough draft and added one more session to make our final decisions. I wanted them to have the wedding of their dreams.

We were just about finished when Jena said, "I left something out. I'd like my father to play his saxophone at the wedding."

"Sounds good," I replied. "Tell me a little bit about what he likes to play and how well he plays."

I tried to be discreet, but I was fishing for what might be coming at the wedding. I've seen some friends and relatives knock their music out of the park. And I've seen some groaners. But it was *their* wedding and whatever they wanted would be fine with me.

She lit up and talked glowingly about her father's abilities. I told her what a great feature it would be at their wedding, her father playing his heart out for his daughter. I warned her about the tears on both sides.

Then she said with excitement, "Where can we put my father in the ceremony? I don't want him doing the prelude. I want everyone to hear him as part of the actual wedding."

"Fine by me," I responded.

And then I looked very seriously and intently at the two of them as I leaned towards them and said, "I only have one stipulation and I won't bend on it." They sobered up and leaned towards me as if to say, *What could be coming?* Then out it came, "What's the stipulation?"

"Well," I said, "Your father has to play his saxophone *after* you take your wedding vows. He won't be permitted to play before that time."

They looked stunned and bewildered. "Why? Why don't you want him to play before we take our vows?"

They were totally unprepared for what I was about to say. "Well," I paused for effect, "we don't allow premarital sax in our church."

The momentary tension was broken with uproarious laughter. They could hardly stop. You could see they felt relieved to know I was only kidding them.

The wedding day arrived, and Dad played his sax. It was an incredible, albeit emotional, solo. And it was *before* the vows, the first ever case of premarital sax in our church.

And while the couple cried during the song, they caught my eye as if to say, "We'll never forget that premarital sax comment as long as we live."

48

THE VEIL

Weddings are always a big, happy event. The couple has worked hard to make their day perfect. Multiple hours and much cash have been invested in the day that will be at the pinnacle of their memories for a lifetime. They hope nothing will go wrong.

Kevin Galvin and Marlene Ferry made a great couple. They were in their mid-twenties and rather mature for their age. They were already experienced in the business world and ready to take on the great adventure of marriage.

We sailed through the premarital counseling sessions. We put the wedding service together. All the arrangements were made. All that remained was the wedding itself.

I run a tight ship at wedding rehearsals as I become the director of a wonderful drama. We practice everything that we'll do the next day, from start to finish, several times. I tell them they don't have to remember a thing the next day. Just watch me.

As I close the rehearsal, we reassemble in the front seats of the Worship Center for my final comments. I talk about things like the time for arrival the next day, the photo shoot, and bringing me the wedding license. I tell them to eat something before they come, because we don't want anyone passing out on an empty stomach. I also inquire as to how long the bride's veil and train will be. I tell the bride's father to be careful and the wedding attendants to assist.

Finally, I tell them that probably something will go wrong in the wedding. Anything can happen including a mistake by me. But I tell the wedding couple that nothing can ruin a wedding. Nothing! Whenever something goes wrong, it may seem like a tragedy at the moment, but it will turn out to be one heck of a funny memory down the road. "Don't panic, don't freak out," is my closing statement. And then I dismiss the party to the rehearsal dinner.

The next day, everyone showed up on time. The wedding party looked awesome. The guests were exuberant. The organ prelude finished. On cue, I led the men's entourage to the front of the church. The ladies began to process down the aisle. Soon everyone was in place and the ceremony began. Marlene's veil and train were majestically long and flowing behind her.

Things were cruising right along. Soon I came to the part in which I say, "Who gives this woman to be married to this man?" The bride's father said, "Her mother and I." He lifted the veil and kissed his daughter. Then he turned and shook Kevin's hand.

I could tell the father was a little nervous and had forgotten about the length of Marlene's veil and train. As he turned to take his seat, he took a step which firmly planted his left foot on the veil and train. Then he brought his right foot through to take another step.

That foot caught Marlene's veil and jerked it from her head like it had been caught with a fish line. It flew at least five feet in the air before it landed. The bride went *Ooh* as her eyes flashed upward. The congregation let out a collective *Ooh* as well.

Marlene turned around to see where her veil had landed. Meanwhile, her father retrieved it and sheepishly did his best to reattach the veil to her head. By now the bride was somewhat unsettled, but she kept her composure. As we continued the ceremony, Marlene would occasionally lift her eyes upward to see if she could assess the damage.

That flying veil struck me as intensely funny. I started to laugh. Totally fearing that I'd lose it, I began to think of every bad thing that ever happened to me. I bit my tongue until it hurt in order to curb the laughter.

When we came to the wedding prayer, the couple knelt before me as I took their hands in mine. My wife began to sing *The Lord's Prayer*. But I couldn't control my laughter anymore. I had kept a lid on it as best I could. As Marie sang, laughter leaked out from me in short, little air gusts. After the solo, it subsided.

We finished the wedding and, as soon as I presented the bride and groom to the congregation, I took off like a rocket for the room behind the platform. I plopped on the sofa and had my catharsis. Marie joined me and it was laughing hyena time.

Marie and I made our way to the reception. When Marie was alone, Marlene came up to her and said, "Your husband has the most tender heart. He cried the whole time he held our hands during your solo." Marie didn't have the heart to tell her what really happened – at least not then.

Eventually, we spilled the beans. They thought it was incredibly funny. And they were so glad I had warned them the night before that something could go wrong in the wedding. It now abides as the funniest moment of that day.

49

THE LAUGHING BOX

I n the early 1990s, our church in Erie, Pennsylvania, underwent a major Worship Center renovation. Ministry can't stop and so we worked around it, including weddings.

Strange things happen at weddings. People pass out. People throw up. People drop rings. Things I can't control.

But *I* never want to be the source of a major *faux pas*, especially at *this* wedding. I was marrying Bill and Shirley Ludwig's daughter. Bill was the Elder Chairman and Shirley the Choir Director. No one knew it, but I felt extra pressure to make this wedding hum. No screw-ups allowed!

I decided to make the church construction situation work for me. When people get married, they begin to construct a home, a relationship that will hopefully last for a lifetime. I thought, *How clever it would be to use the church building under construction as a reference point for talking about the construction of their marriage.*

We breezed through premarital counseling. This couple was mature. They planned everything to perfection. They were ready.

The rehearsal night came, and it went flawlessly. Everyone knew their cues and placements. I thought, *This is a prelude to a perfect wedding.*

169

As 2:00 pm arrived on the wedding day, all systems were go. The right people were in the right places. The guests were being ushered in. The weather was perfect.

The groom, Jim Bachinsky, and I, along with the groomsmen, made our way to the front of the church. The processional began. Cindy Ludwig, the bride, finally appeared. She was resplendent in a gorgeous gown. There was an air of anticipation along with some sniffles throughout the congregation.

Soon the bride, her father, and the wedding party stood before me. The wedding began to unfold flawlessly – its special music, Scripture reading, the pledges, the giving of the bride.

The time for the sermon arrived. I started out, "This will not be your normal, serious wedding. I just want to prepare you ahead of time." I had no idea how prophetic those words would be.

I continued, "Your wedding has taken on somewhat of a construction subplot. Our church is under construction, and yours is the last wedding during this disruption."

To underscore the construction theme, I brought along a toolbox. I told the couple that I put some tools in the box that would help them construct their new home. "You can have what's inside the box and as I speak, I'll show you a tool for each point."

The sermon had five one-word points that all began with the letter "L." How appropriate. The bride's last name was Ludwig. "Each of these tools will help you build a strong home."

I began with "Language." The tool I showed them was some duct tape to cover their mouths if their language ever began to tear down rather than build up. Point Three was "Labor." Point Four was "Love." And Point Five was "Lordship." Each point had an appropriate tool.

It was Point Two that occasioned the disruption in this story.

This couple loved to laugh, especially the bride. I told them how many couples start out laughing but when things get tough, they start crying. "Laughter is like a good medicine," I said, "even in troubling circumstances."

And then I showed them their tool. It was a laughing box. "When you've lost your sense of humor, pick up this tool." I gave the box a little jolt. It responded with its infectious laugh. The bride and groom laughed. So did the wedding party. So did the church. The father of the bride looked a little skeptical. But I thought, *How clever! This really went over well.*

I put the laughing box on the platform floor to the side near a floral bouquet and proceeded to finish the sermon. The time came for the wedding party to ascend the three steps to the platform. It was there that the vows would be given.

We made our ascent starting with me. The bride and groom followed. So did the wedding party.

Then something went drastically wrong.

As the groomsmen made their way up the steps, one of them nudged the laughing box. My worst fears came to pass. At the most serious moment of the wedding, the laughing box was out of control and there was nothing I could do. Awkward laughter rippled through the congregation. The wedding couple looked at each other and smiled but you could tell they were also wondering, *Where is this heading?*

And the father of the bride? Bill didn't look amused. I thought, *He's going to kill me for ruining Cindy's wedding.* I broke out in a profuse sweat as the wedding party reassembled before me on the platform. A solemn moment had become next to a comedy.

There was no way that I could leave my post and turn off the laughing box. After what seemed like an eternity, it finally stopped.

The wedding proceeded without any additional hitches. But I knew what was coming. What goes up must come down. At the end of the ceremony, the wedding party would bound down the wedding steps triumphantly and retreat down the aisle. Would one of those guys trigger that laughing box again? I was in a panic mode. I prayed earnestly to God. I wanted a future in the church.

It was as though a miracle happened. I said, "It's my pleasure to present to you for the first time, Mr. and Mrs. Jim Bachinsky." Immediately the recessional music began to play, *Saddle up your horses. We've got a trail to blaze.* Out went the bride and groom followed by the rambunctious wedding party. That laughing box never made a sound!

Relief swept across me. I was extremely sorry for the mishap. But it could have been a disaster.

I retrieved the box, turned it off, and put it in my possession. I wasn't going to have anyone playing with it.

When the wedding party and family members returned to the platform for pictures, the laughing box was gone. I was in the clear. But I apologized profusely to the father and mother of the bride.

They graciously granted me an umbrella of mercy. The wedding couple thought it was hilarious.

At the reception, I gave the newlyweds the tool I had withheld – their laughing box. I told them that there was no way they wouldn't belly laugh every time they heard it. "But do me a favor," I cautioned them. "Don't use this when your father's around!"

Fortunately for me, it became a funny memory for him as well. And things went just fine in future Elder Board meetings.

50

THE BATS

We never outgrow some fears. Bats is one for me.

It was common to have an intrusive bat flying inside the home of my youth. We lived in an old row house and they'd find their way through the tiniest orifices of our slate roof. They'd get into our attic only to find their way into our bedrooms at night. I'd scream and then jump under the bed while Dad fearlessly solved the invasion with a broom.

Fortunately, bats never found their way into our marital abode. But at times, I found evidence of bats on our front porch floor. There were droppings from behind the second-floor shutters and on occasion, I could hear their squeaks. It would raise hackles on the back of my neck. The bats had to go and Dad wasn't around.

I concocted a plan. I got the water hose and sprayed water upwards into the shutters. I wasn't sure if the bat would come dive-bombing in my direction as I fought back fear. But I took the chance. It wasn't long until a drowned bat fell to the porch floor. With gloves, I cautiously picked up the glass jar I brought for confining him and with a garden tool, I dropped him in.

With tightened lid, the jar was ready for disposal when I got a devious idea. *Take it to the church office and put it in the freezer. When my secretary, Lois Nelson, opens the door, she'll have a surprise waiting for her.* Now, why would a bat-averse guy take to an idea like this? Only one reason: his teasing side.

By the way, Lois had a scream you could hear across the county.

A day or so later, I was in my office when I heard a scream that could only mean one thing – Lois had found the bat. I ran to her side to console her. Shaking and with a frown, she finally accepted my apology. Fortunately, our working and friendship relationship survived.

But my antics continued. We were on a family vacation in Austin, Texas in 1998. Marie's relatives took us to see a bat display unlike any other in the world. I was reluctant as they took us to a perfect spot near the Congress Avenue Bridge to view what happens every night at dusk. One and a half million bats fly out from beneath the bridge in a massive, dark cloud into the nighttime sky. Many of them fly too low for comfort.

I was standing behind my daughter, Rachel, when I responded to a sudden impulse. As some of the bats seemed to dive-bomb us, I took a sheet of paper and rattled it over her head, slightly touching her hair. Her screamed rivaled that of Lois. Unfortunately, it took a little longer for Rachel to forgive me than it did for Lois.

Fast forward years later. What goes around comes around.

I was at an intense women's weekend retreat as a Spiritual Director in Erie. We were in required lockdown from Friday night at 6:00pm until 6:00pm on Sunday night. There was only one other male in the mix, a fellow Spiritual Director, Joel Marks.

Friday evening was full of activities and group sessions. As the evening waned, we settled into the main room for our final group session of the night. The ladies were in groups of seven around tables and the leaders of the retreat sat at a head table.

It was just after 10:00pm when a commotion ensued in the middle of the room. The women started to duck and dodge as they screamed, "A bat! A bat!" Suddenly the airborne creature seemed everywhere at once.

What did the man fearful of bats who liked to tease others do? I dove under the table, and there I stayed. I don't know where Joel went but he wasn't much help either. But one of the brave lady leaders came to the rescue. She calmly took charge of the chaos and was able to open a door to the outside. The bat finally departed.

My heroics didn't go unnoticed. The ladies started to tease me incessantly as they chanted, "Our hero! Our hero!" For the rest of the weekend, the ladies spoke of my heroism with a twinkle in their eyes and a grin on their faces. And me? I was embarrassed and couldn't believe I had left my command and fled under a table, leaving them all vulnerable to attack.

When awards were given out at the end of the retreat, they included me. I was given a battery-operated furry bat for my office. There it stayed for over a year as I explained my heroism to anyone who would ask, "Why the bat?" Eventually I gave it to one of my grandkids at Halloween minus the story about Pop Pop's "heroism."

Heroes come in many stripes and colors. In this instance, mine happened to be yellow. I'm certain that Lois and Rachel felt justice was served.

Postscript:

I've changed my position on bats. I'm still afraid of them. But they're not threatening pests that get rabies. They play a vital role in our ecosystem. They eat millions of pounds of insects and save billions of dollars in pest control services. Plus, they pollinate over 700 kinds of plants, some of which we use for food and medicine.

These days bats are welcome at my house - we're just not close friends.

51

HOSPITAL CAPERS

One hope looms large when you go to a hospital: *please, don't let the doctor make a mistake!* But mistakes happen. They're just more tolerable when pastors make them.

I've had my share of hospital mistakes over the years. I've seen other pastors make them too. Fortunately, no one has died as a result – although some have come close to dying from laughter!

Part of my pastoral ministry is praying for a patient in the hospital before surgery. Usually, surgery is scheduled early in the morning. I'm not a morning person, but duty calls.

Fresh out of seminary, Howard Horras was my very first patient. I had just arrived as a new pastor at my first church in the Chicago area, and I barely knew him. Early in the morning before surgery, I went to the hospital to pray with him. Following surgery, in the late afternoon, I decided to go back and check on him.

No one told me what to expect when I was admitted into the ICU. There before me was an unconscious man with every wire, tube, and monitor imaginable in, on, and around him. It was horrific!

Suddenly, I felt light-headed and a little unsteady on my feet. A staff person came to my side to see about my well-being. I took a deep breath, steadied myself, and offered a speedy prayer. I thought they were going to offer me a bed. I left that room wondering if I had been in Frankenstein's lab. Things have drastically changed since 1975. They want you up and walking on the second day after surgery!

* * *

In 1978, we moved to Grace Baptist Church in Erie, Pennsylvania. As Senior Pastor, hospital visitation was a major part of my ministry. Sometimes during those visits, the serious became funny.

Once, when surgery was scheduled for someone at 7:00 am, I arose extra early while it was still dark. I decided to dress without turning on the lights so as not to disturb Marie. Mission accomplished, I sped to the hospital. Four people got on the elevator with me. At one point or another, each of them looked down and then looked up at me with a faint grin. No one spoke a word. I'm thinking, *Quiet but friendly people so early in the morning.*

When I got to the patient's room, I noticed that the family of the patient had gathered around his bed. Interns would be arriving for him momentarily so we gathered in a little circle by the bed, heads bowed in prayer. When the prayer ended, the same thing happened. Everyone looked up at me with a faint grin.

Before I headed out the door, a relative pulled me aside and asked, "Pastor, do you know that you have two different shoes on?" I looked down to see one black and one brown shoe. My face flushed red and, instantly, I realized that half the world knew about my shoes before I did. When I told Marie, she pleaded with me, "Turn on some lights from now on! I doubt that you'll set enviable fashion trends by dressing in the dark!"

* * *

On another occasion, I was running late to the hospital, and my mind was distracted with a thousand other thoughts. I asked the lady at the Information Desk for Cathy Froehlich's room number.

It was on the maternity floor. When the elevator door opened, there was a big mural on the wall. It was a stork with a baby and sack in its beak. It said, "Welcome to Baby Land."

I knew why I was there; Cathy just had a hysterectomy. But with my distractions and all the images and babies on the maternity floor, I had a lapse. I arrived at Cathy's room and cheerfully inquired, "Is it a boy or a girl?"

Soberly Cathy exclaimed, "Pastor, I had a hysterectomy!" I fell all over myself with apologies. I was fearful that she thought me incompetent. But doing my best to explain my blunder, she was more than ready to forgive. I think my red face helped. In a moment, we were both laughing.

* * *

The day came when my secretary, Lois Nelson, needed surgery. As is my custom, I went to the hospital to pray with her. Her entire in-town family was present in the room. We talked a little about the upcoming surgery and I engaged in some humorous chit-chat with her family. Soon it was time for prayer.

Before I prayed, words came out of my mouth I never expected to say.

"You know, Lois, this is a pretty routine operation. But sometimes things go wrong. If you don't come out of this, at least you know where you'll be."

Lois's lower lip began to quiver while her family cracked up, questioning my brand of comfort. I backpedaled and prayed. Too late. Lois was in tears. But it became a funny memory for years to come.

* * *

Eventually it was *my* turn for surgery. I told my church leaders, "No need to come to the hospital for prayer that early, I'll cover it myself." I was, however, grateful for Marie's prayer. Unlike my words to Lois, Marie said that I'd do just fine.

I never come out of anesthesia well; I get extremely nauseated. Such was the case in the hospital shower when I fell to my knees. I pulled the alarm string for help.

Marie said, "But you're naked!"

My response: "I don't care if the whole world sees me, I'm so sick." Two nurses rushed in; I couldn't have cared less.

Shortly thereafter, I was woozy in bed when one of the nurses came to my side. "How are you doing?" she asked.

"I'm shake and weaky." Marie began to chuckle.

And then, continuing in my foggy state, "I'm Pastor Al from Grace Church and I'd like to invite you to one of our services." She smiled and left. Marie quipped, "She'll probably never come after what she saw in the shower room." Marie was right.

* * *

It was a busy Friday afternoon at Hamot Hospital. I boarded the first-floor elevator with six other people. The car lifted with a jerk, went a few feet, and stopped. Most of us have ridden a cranky elevator at some point. It usually continues on its way. This time it didn't.

There was silence in the elevator as we all analyzed what was going on. We gave it about a minute. Nothing happened. "Houston, I think we have a problem," I finally said, as I rang the emergency buzzer.

We want everything instantly in our society – computers, fast food, pictures, banking, and well, elevators. We all expected to be free as a bird in a few minutes. Nothing happened. It was before cell phone days, and we were cut off from communication. We had no idea what was going on. Minutes passed and no rescue.

As time went on, it was getting stuffy. We couldn't sit down. There was little room to move. Fifteen minutes turned into thirty. No rescue. The occupants were surprisingly civil.

I finally said, "Tell you what. Let me share a little about me and what I'm doing here." Another person followed suit. And then another. We all took turns. Perfect strangers were becoming instant, albeit temporary, friends. There was no panic. It was team building.

After forty-five minutes, the elevator moved and returned to the first floor. As the door opened, we all said, "Thank God!" followed by, "Glad to meet you."

And then I said, "How about a reunion next year?" We all laughed and parted ways, never to see each other again. A little bit of humor and a whole lot of friendliness prevented what could have been a very panicky situation.

* * *

One of my friends was in for a heart procedure at St. Vincent's Hospital. I found him in his room on the cardiac floor. We chatted for a while, I prayed, and then I left. On my way out, I passed a big sign on the hall wall. It said, *Be careful. Heart* **morality** *rises when these five conditions are present.* It listed the five.

Heart morality! It was the funniest sign I'd ever seen in a hospital and enough to give a pastor a hearty laugh. At least it was better than what Larry Lewis, a youth speaker friend of mine, said in California before hundreds at an outdoor youth rally I attended.

He read *I Corinthians 15:53* this way, *For this perishable body must put on the imperishable, and this mortal body must put on* **immorality.**

Immediately he said, "Oh boy!" The crowd went crazy with laughter, but he had sure gained their attention.

One letter can change everything!

52

FUNERAL TALES

D ead men tell no tales. But live ones do.

Being in the ministry for nearly fifty years, I've encountered a lot of true funeral tales. I've discovered that often humor lies *buried* – excuse the pun! – in many situations.

Some things are never funny at funerals because of the severity of the tragedy. Other things are funny only after time goes by. And some things are funny at the very moment they happen. It's to this latter category to which I now turn.

* * *

One funeral over which I presided took place on a cold, rainy day. Arriving at the cemetery, I asked the funeral director where the head of the casket was. He directed me and I stepped close to the casket. A grass-like tarp covered the ground as it draped away from the coffin and grave.

I thought the earth was solid beneath it but, unbeknownst to anyone, water had eroded some of the soil. As I stepped towards the casket, my left foot slipped into the depression. My leg started to enter the

FUNERAL TALES

grave between the sidewall and the casket. The funeral director quickly grabbed me and rescued the day. One foot in the grave took on new meaning for me!

* * *

Sometimes we have funerals at the church. One of our staff custodians, Debbie Lundberg, struggled every time that happened. She has a fear of being alone in the presence of the deceased.

One day, a body was brought to the church for the viewing. It would stay in the viewing room overnight. The church needed to be opened early the next morning for the funeral.

Debbie came early to open the building. As she walked away from the body and down a dark hallway, I came out of an adjacent door right behind her. I was reluctant to say, "Hi, Debbie," for fear of scaring her. So I put out my hand and gently laid it on her shoulder to signal my presence. Wrong choice.

Screaming in horror, she jumped several feet in the air, and bolted towards the office, leaping down a short flight of stairs. She promptly threw herself headlong onto the office sofa and clutched her heart. She was as white as a sheet. I pled innocence but Debbie wasn't having it. I honestly wanted to avoid scaring her, but it backfired. That was the week we almost had two funerals.

* * *

It was a cold January morning with snow, high winds, and an 8-degree temperature. Early in my ministry, I donned a fedora for funerals. My associate, Dave Snyder, was a tall man and stood by my side that day.

The funeral director began the graveside service with these remarks, "Gentlemen, you will not disrespect the dead if you keep your hats on."

183

With one hand I had been holding my hat on my head for fear of it blowing off with the high winds. But I needed both hands to hold my Bible and notes. I was on the horns of a dilemma when I whispered to Dave, "Would you please hold my hat?" He immediately replied, "No."

Startled, I thought, *How could there be such insubordination at a time like this?*

Turns out that we had two different ideas of what "holding my hat" meant. I wanted to take it off my head and have Dave hold it. He thought that I wanted him to take his hands and hold the hat on my head while I officiated.

Communication can be defined as "the meeting of meanings." Our meanings never met that day as I struggled to keep my hat on.

* * *

Sometimes we cover many miles in the funeral lead car on the way to the cemetery. It gives an opportunity for me to talk with the funeral director. Jack Botwright and I would get into some good conversations. Oh, the stories he would tell.

Jack has a heavy foot. He had to transport a body in his hearse from Erie to downstate Pennsylvania on the Interstate. The speed limit in those days was 55 mph and he wanted to make the round trip as fast as he could.

He was almost at his destination. The exit ramp was in sight when he looked in his rear-view mirror. The squad car lights were on, and Jack knew he was the target. "Darn," he said. "I was almost there."

I asked Jack some questions. *Did the officer know you were transporting a body? Did you expect him to treat a funeral director, with a body in his hearse, with a little latitude? Did he give you a warning or a ticket?* Jack said, "The guy was all business. He didn't care what the situation was. He wrote me up for $165."

I was somewhat surprised that the officer didn't give Jack any professional courtesy. And I couldn't resist some dry humor. "Wow, Jack! I'd call that a stiff fine."

For a moment, I thought he'd veer off the road in laughter. After weaving a bit, Jack checked his rear-view mirror. There were no flashing lights.

* * *

Some years ago, my daughter-in-law's father, Jim Luke, died suddenly in his sleep. He was only in his fifties. The viewing lines were long, and the family received guests nonstop from 1pm to 11pm. The next morning, there was standing room only for the funeral.

The pastor began his sermon. He was going a tad long, but under the circumstances, understandable. We knew he was about to finish when he said, "In closing…." But he went on. Again he said, "In closing…," But he went on. A third time he said, "In closing…," and he continued on.

That's when a person behind me leaned over to his friend and said, "When is this guy ever going to shut up?" I chuckled and thought to myself, *He said what we were all thinking. That's why I have brief sermons at funerals. I want to quit when people want more, not when they want me to shut up.*

When the pastor said, "Amen," there was a sigh behind me that ended with the word, "Finally!"

* * *

Our church administrator, Dick Page, drove an old, disintegrating station wagon. It was so ugly everyone teased him about it. Even my children would say, "Dad, when is Pastor Dick going to get a new car?" The day finally arrived when he announced that he was buying another car. Everyone cheered, including my kids.

By common consensus, we decided that we needed a funeral for that old rattletrap. The entire staff and a few relatives gathered in the Worship Center. I presided. The service had every feature contained in a standard funeral – opening remarks, Scripture, eulogies and sharing, a PowerPoint picture video, a message, and weeping throughout. The station wagon sat near the church doorway for one last viewing.

After about thirty sorrowful minutes, the service was over and the car was rolled out of sight. We commiserated with Dick and his family and then adjourned to the Fellowship Hall for a funeral dinner. Suddenly, the sorrowful tone dissipated, and the place turned into a royal hoot.

I've done hundreds of funerals, but this was my one and only car funeral. It put the "fun" in "funeral!"

53

CAMP CAPERS

Family camp at Camp Burton, Ohio, was a big tradition for many families in our church in the 1980s and 90s. As many as twenty families would spend a memorable week together.

Throughout the day, there were plenty of activities for the entire family. At night, the adults had a special track as they met together for singing and a message from the family camp pastor. The kids had their own meeting with the camp staff.

Afterward, we'd put the kids to bed, and the adults would play games until two in the morning. Euchre and Canasta were the big hits. As we'd make our way back to the cabins in the wee hours of the morning, we'd likely see a couple of skunks lurking in the shadows. They must have been Christian skunks, because they never sprayed.

We got to know each other well over the course of the week. And that included playing pranks on people. I happened to be a target of one of the pranks.

As camp pastor, I had special accommodations in the guest speaker cabin. It contained a bedroom, a little living room/kitchen combination, a bathroom, and a small loft.

One night, while others played games, I went to my cabin to use the bathroom in preparation for bed. It had been a long, full day of fun and excitement, and I was tired. In the privacy of my bathroom, I wasn't prepared for what was about to happen.

As I approached the toilet, the lid was down. I thought it strange, because I never put the lid down. Standing before the toilet, preparing to use it, I lifted the lid. Immediately, something jumped up at me like a bolt of lightning. It scared me to my core.

It landed on my foot, and I screamed in horror. I was afraid to see what it was but with an involuntary reflex, I kicked and looked at the same time. It was a huge toad. He must have been waiting hours for someone to free him.

The bathroom window was a crank style with hinges at the top. It would open on an angle. Outside and underneath the window were voyeurs Bill Wiltse and Eric Rhodes. They must have waited, who knows how long, for their victim to use the bathroom. Of course, the angle of the window only magnified my scream.

They couldn't control themselves. They erupted in spontaneous laughter, and I heard the shuffle as they scampered away into the dark. With hackles on my back I yelled, "God's going to get you!" It took a while for me to recover before I retired for the night. I kept reliving the "leap" and my total and fearful reaction. Eventually I fell asleep.

The next morning, I entered the dining hall. People were at the breakfast tables and all eyes were indirectly upon me, but no one was owning up to anything. "Is anyone jumpy this morning?" I said. Some ripples of laughter. "Does the word 'toadstool' mean anything to you?" More laughter, but no one came forward. It took several days until the well-meaning culprits admitted their sin.

That morning, when breakfast was served, my friend Scott Crossman saw a piece of French toast on the food line that looked like it had mold on it. Of course, it was his imagination. But he wouldn't take it. Before the meal was over, I retrieved that piece of French toast and placed it in a plastic cereal bowl. I had plans for it.

Family camp was long over when Scott's birthday arrived. I put the dish of mangy French toast in a box and beautifully wrapped it. I asked his wife, Miriam, to take the gift home and give it to him. Neither knew what was in the gift box, but it was quite a hoot when Scott opened it.

At Christmas, there was a special gift from Scott under our tree. It was that bowl and French toast, now laden with real mold and worse for the wear. That bowl and French toast found its way back and forth between Scott and me over the years. Sometimes there were long intervals, because we'd lose track of it and then find it again.

Scott wanted to return the French toast to me, but he couldn't find it. So he did the incredible. He drove to Camp Burton, 75 miles one way. The dining hall was locked, but he wouldn't be denied. Finding a way to open a window, he climbed in, securing another cereal bowl and slice of French toast. So much for camp security.

One Sunday morning, it happened to be my birthday. I used to sit in a special chair on the Worship Center platform every Sunday. As I approached my chair, there was this beautifully wrapped gift sitting on my seat. I opened the card, *To Pastor Al from your loving congregation.* I was moved. But suddenly, I had this suspicion that something wasn't quite right. Instead of opening the gift right there and thanking the congregation, I put it aside to open after the service. My instincts saved me. It was that crazy bowl and French toast.

Scott reveled knowing that he almost got me really good. After the service, he told me the replacement story about his trek to camp. I nearly doubled over in laughter.

The French toast and bowl made a few more circuits and then it disappeared again. I think Scott has it, and he thinks I have it. It's been gone for years. But I wouldn't be surprised to see that old and rotting piece of French toast show up again. If it doesn't, it wouldn't be out of the question for Scott to raid the camp kitchen one more time.

54

THE SQUIRREL

Comedian and singer Ray Stevens sang a song years ago about the day the squirrel went berserk in the First Self-Righteous Church. Little did I think a squirrel would cause a stir in my own dear congregation.

I had just come from pastoring in the northern suburbs of Chicago. That church had been built in the 1960's and was without air conditioning. Services in the summertime were sweltering, so air conditioning was finally added.

So here I was, at Grace Church in Erie, Pennsylvania, and it seemed like it was back to square one for me. Our Worship Center was fairly new at the time (predating my arrival there) and, for some reason, the building committee had decided against air conditioning. Sunday after Sunday throughout the summer, the faithful sweated it out. The only available remedy involved large ceiling fans and oscillating fans at the front side aisles of the Worship Center, with every available door wide open.

One hot Sunday, we had a guest speaker. In those days, the Senior Pastor never left the platform. When he wasn't standing behind the pulpit, he was sitting in his special chair. And the organist, Janet Barns?

Once the music portion of the service was over, she sat in a little booth at the front of the Worship Center, next to the organ.

The guest preacher was well into his sermon. I was sitting uncomfortably in my chair when, suddenly, I heard to my right a loud, anguished, crescendoing, "Oh! No! OH! NO!" It was Janet, crying out in the middle of the sermon. For a second, I thought she was being uncharacteristically moved by the Spirit.

I looked to my left and there it was – a squirrel moving stealthily toward Janet along the wall. It had come in the back door adjacent to the platform. Janet waited as long as she could before her exclamations. Now she was convinced the squirrel was coming for her.

I rose and put my hand on the preacher's shoulder. He paused, and I said, "Time out. We've got a visitor." Because his back was to the proceedings, he had no idea what was going on. But the church had already noticed and was getting restless.

Suddenly, the squirrel turned on a dime. It left its route toward Janet and took a sharp left into the congregation. There was screaming and hollering and jumping like I'd never seen at church. It would have put a Pentecostal meeting to shame.

There was nothing I could do but watch. I'd pay admission to see it all over again. That squirrel ran back and forth under the pews in random and unpredictable patterns while the people ran or stood on pews to get out of the way. It looked like a field of wheat waving back and forth in a strong wind.

We had block walls, wooden beams, and a vaulted wooden ceiling. Suddenly, the squirrel left the floor and ran up the block wall. It could only get so far up the smooth beams until it fell back to the floor in the middle of the screaming congregants. It happened several times, while the people covered their heads and squealed.

The ushers swung into action. Grabbing brooms from the janitor's closet, they chased after that squirrel. I could tell that the congregation was skeptical of their efforts.

Just as it looked like the people were about to flee the Worship Center, the squirrel ran through the sanctuary doors into the lobby and out the main doors to the parking lot.

The congregation was abuzz for several minutes before I could quiet them down. In utter relief, laughter began to prevail. I don't know how he did it but, after I reintroduced the preacher and made some comical remarks, he finished his sermon.

Those who were in that service will never forget the day the squirrel went berserk in our church. It wasn't like the Ray Steven's song where the squirrel ran up the leg of Harry's britches and Sister Bertha Better-Than-You cried out to *confess sins that would make a sailor blush* when it ran up her dress.

But there was enough whoopin' and hollerin' for Stevens to have written a sequel about a squirrel that went berserk in the Grace Squirrel-Frightened Church.

By the way, it wasn't too long until somebody in the church paid to have air conditioning installed. We were soon able to worship in comfort without the threat of another squirrel on the loose.

55

"AL"ISMS

A drian Rogers was the Senior Pastor of the Bellevue Baptist Church in Memphis, Tennessee for 33 years and three-time president of the Southern Baptist Convention. He was a gifted preacher and, under his leadership, his church grew to 29,000.

Adrian never preached a boring sermon. Each was anointed and powerful, dripping with wisdom and wit. He was a master at turning a phrase and, like Solomon, he spoke countless wise sayings and expressions, both original and borrowed. These were such a gold mine that they were collected into a book called *Adrianisms*.

Some examples include: "What's down in the well comes up in the bucket," and "We need to be humbly grateful and not grumbly hateful," and "We ought to live like Jesus died yesterday, rose this morning, and is coming back this afternoon."

I was the Senior Pastor of Grace Church in Erie, Pennsylvania, for 32 years. The church grew to 1000. I was never in the league of Adrian, not even close. But I too spoke many sayings and expressions over the years that became known as "Al"isms.

But there's a big difference. My "Al"isms were not well-crafted wit and wisdom; they came out amusingly wrong or awkward.

Most of my "Al"isms were spoken in front of my church and church staff. They were so enamored with my miscues that many of them are etched permanently in their memories. My secretary Kathy Herrmann kept an "Al"ism journal. I credit her with many of the ones that follow.

I've provided the precipitating circumstance followed by the "Al"ism. All the "Al"isms were well-meant and unintentional. They span many years with amazing frequency.

Here we go:

Adding to the discussion in a staff meeting: "Let me piggy tail on that."

When *MySpace* and *Facebook* first came out and I was clueless: "Could someone please explain *My Face* to me."

It was time for some of our staff to get in the van to travel to a conference: "It's time to go. Let's mount the van."

When one of our plans went awry: "This will throw us into a monkey wrench."

When I was certain that a difficult challenge would be easy: "That will be a dam slunk." When it wasn't: "We're going to get our noose in a neck."

This inversion of letters and words continued: "Lo and Melis" for Lois and Mel, "Bill and Jernie" for Jill and Bernie, "light of boltning" for bolt of lightning, and "switch and bait" for bait and switch.

Even though I always meant well, I fared particularly poorly in the pregnancy department:

- To Melanie Deppen in a green dress during the Christmas season: "You look like a Christmas tree. You know, wide at the bottom."
- To Jen Gingrich, "You look like you swallowed a watermelon."
- To Heather Newton, "When are you due?" Answer: "Four months." Me: "Four months! It looks like any day!"
- Visiting my Executive Pastor's wife, Kim Sanford, a few days after delivery: "Are you going to join the Weigh-Down workshop?"

When a pastor friend was having a hard time in his church: "He'll be flying with a limp."

When praying before surgery for the Lord's protection for Miriam Crossman on our staff: "Lord, take her."

One day I took something to Sandy Nelson's house. She opened the front door and said, "My hair is wet because I just got out of the shower." The next time I saw Sandy was in our church office when I said: "Last time I saw you, you were just getting out of the shower."

Some of our staff were around the break table, the day following a little staff excursion in my car, when I said to Miriam Crossman: "Don't forget! You left your sweater in the back seat of my car."

When I had a bad cold: "I can't hear you. My tubes are tied."

When I felt strongly about an issue but felt someone on staff was more qualified: "We need to take a stand here, and I'm not the one to do it."

When my secretary Annie Watson was collecting money for a church event: "Annie's an honest person. She'll take your money."

Lois Nelson was my secretary for 17 years. At her church retirement party, I was speaking about her replacement. "I have a protective principle," I said. "I never hire an attractive or good-looking secretary." I had a lot of explaining to do on that one.

After looking for one of my staff ladies at church: "I've been looking you all over" but meant "I've been looking all over for you."

When accompanying my fearful and timid senior citizen custodian, Evelyn Singleton, to her court hearing after an accident: "If they put you in jail, I'll come visit you."

After our church made a donation for a school fundraiser, this could have come out better: "They actually think we have a heart for the community."

In commenting about being in a bookstore: "I was browsing for books at Baskin and Robbins (the ice cream store instead of Barnes and Noble)."

When my family was visiting Presque Isle State Park on a hot summer day and a car of guys whistled and shouted at Marie: "Nice legs!" I shouted back, to my family's surprise: "You wouldn't know nice legs if you saw them!"

And so it goes.

I know where my "Al"isms come from. My dad. It was part of who he was. His name was Al as well. Even with all the years since his untimely death in 1995, my family and those who knew him still rehearse them.

Here's a classic. Dad was about to drive a truck out of state for several days. His wife (my stepmother Lillie) was holding their dog in the living room, bidding Dad goodbye as he headed for the door.

"Aren't you forgetting something?" inquired Lillie.

"Oh yes. Goodbye, Prince," and he walked over and kissed the dog goodbye. Lillie never got her kiss, but she understood my dad and his "Al"isms.

How thankful I am that my family and former staff understand mine!

56

THE NON-ACCIDENT ACCIDENT

My father taught me how to drive a stick shift in a '51 Plymouth on the back roads of farming country thirty miles north of Philadelphia. I was twelve. It was no surprise then that I passed my driver's exam with flying colors at sixteen. Soon after, I was on the road in my dad's new 1964 Dodge Dart, the lone car of the family.

Driving was my second love. At nineteen, I was hiking rental cars from downtown Chicago to the O'Hare Airport and back for Budget Rent-a-Car. When I was twenty-one, I drove Chicago Transit Authority commuter buses all over Chicago for two summers while regular drivers vacationed. In winter, it was Chicago Yellow Taxi cabs. Not bad for a guy who grew up in a lazy, little rural town of 5000.

Married at twenty-one, I was the primary driver. In fact, Marie didn't even have a license. With my professional driving background in Chicago, I felt more than qualified to teach her how to drive. She came through with flying colors.

We crisscrossed the States many times during moves and family vacations. I've often wondered how many miles I've logged in my life.

It was hardly a challenge then when David Snell and his wife, Kim, drove up to our house one snowy, February morning. David offered, "How'd you like to drive my new car?" It was one of the first front-wheel drive cars to come out. I'd never driven one, but I was confident of my abilities.

We had planned to go together to attend Founder's Week, a spiritual life conference at Moody Bible Institute in Chicago. Marie and I climbed into the front seats. David and Kim retreated to the rear seats. I adjusted my seat, checked out the dashboard, and adjusted the mirrors.

I was ready to go.

The weather forecast wasn't great, but we were seasoned Erie, Pennsylvania, snow travelers. The falling white stuff receded to the back of our minds except for one little reminder from David as I backed out of our driveway. "Be careful. I just got this car and changed insurance companies. My agent said, 'Don't have an accident.'"

No pressure there! But I wasn't worried.

By the time we approached Cleveland, the roads were incredibly slick. Spun-out cars and trucks littered the landscape. I couldn't help thinking, *This is crazy!* I wasn't the only one in the car with that thought. Conditions worsened. More slip-sliding. The brake wasn't all that effective. No one spoke. We pressed on toward Chicago.

Progress slowed to a crawl through the I-90 downtown S-curve in Cleveland. Expertly maneuvered, my confidence increased. Stopping now was not an option.

On the other side of Cleveland, in morning rush-hour traffic, I suddenly lost control of the car. I did doughnut spins across three lanes of traffic. Somehow, I missed hitting all the cars and trucks around me and escaped the roadside concrete barriers. It reminded me of the time God parted the Red Sea for the Israelites as they escaped from Egypt. We experienced an entire accident minus the crash.

I caught Kim's expression in the rear-view mirror while it was happening. Her head was lowered, fingers touching her furrowed brow. *We're going to die!* her expression seemed to say. I also caught the expression on David's face – calm and relaxed, like nothing was happening.

The car slid to a stop near the center median, perpendicular to oncoming traffic. The engine had died. I only had a second to restart the car and park cleanly on the median. We nervously looked at each other in silent relief. No one could believe we had escaped a certain crash. My nerves took over. First, I laughed uncontrollably. Then I cried.

When we finally had a window of escape through traffic, we decided to take the first exit, find a motel, and proceed to Chicago the next day. Wise choice. En route to the exit, we observed multiple accidents – *actual* accidents.

We found a motel, checked in, and settled down, exhaustion and relief spreading over three of us. But David never seemed to be rattled throughout the whole ordeal. I was still shaking so I had to ask, "David, how could you be so calm and relaxed during our spin-out on the Interstate while the rest of us were scared to death?"

I wasn't ready for his response. "I was with my pastor. I figured that God wasn't going to let anything happen to you, so the rest of us had nothing to worry about." David's theology wasn't quite right. God doesn't give pastors an exemption from accidents. But that day, you couldn't have told David otherwise, and I didn't want to.

I breathed a sigh of relief. Not only had we escaped a terrible accident, David never had to call his insurance agent.

It took me the rest of the day to settle down, and I needed some comic relief. Years later, I still remember the movie we watched in the motel room that day – Jerry Lewis in *The Nutty Professor*.

The next morning, we started out again for Chicago.

"David," I directed. "Marie and I will be in the back seats." There was no objection from him.

Over the years, I've passed that spot on I-90 scores of times. I still marvel that we escaped tragedy, and I send up a prayer of thanks to God. And then I check my rear view mirror. In my mind, I see David sitting in the back seat, cool as a cucumber.

For a moment, I was his rock-solid safe haven.

57

THE NAME BLUNDER

Church members love to laugh at a pastor's slip-ups. Unless, that is, it involves *their* name or the name of someone close to them, as in a funeral. In *that* case it might take a little longer for them to see the humor in it. But truth be told, laypeople don't often realize just how many names we pastors must remember.

I'm fairly good with names. At the same time, I'm fairly bad with names. When I'm on the platform in church or caught off guard and need to call the names of people I know well, I sometimes go blank. Then there are times I not only go blank, I fill in the blank with the wrong name, as you'll see in this story.

Rock and roll was my thing in the 1960's. However, with the advent of flamboyant rock bands in the 1970's and my concentration on studies in seminary, I lost touch with pop culture. I knew some names of artists and bands out there, but not much more.

In the mid 1970's, I graduated from seminary and went into my first ministry. The position I took you never hear of these days – Youth and C.E. (Christian Education) Director. My job description had me major in youth and minor in adult education.

Skokie Valley Baptist Church was in Wilmette, Illinois, in the northern suburbs of Chicago. There were about 30 committed teens in the youth group. A good fit existed between the youth group and me, the youth sponsors and me, and the parents and me. Before long, we all knew each other well, and the ministry went into high gear.

As a young guy fresh out of seminary, my passion was to teach and disciple youth. Sometimes I was too heavy on the teaching part. Fortunately, the youth group was rather forgiving. And sometimes I was clueless about their culture. They had some things to teach *me*.

One time some students were talking about a big concert coming to Chicago. They were going to hear Pink Floyd. To which I responded, "Who's he?" I got a crash course. They were a psychedelic English rock band of five guys.

At the same time, Alice Cooper was big on the rock scene. When some of the youth talked about going to his concert, I asked, "Who's she?" I got another crash course. From that point on, what I knew about *him* was his raspy voice, long hair, and love for shocking his audiences.

I left the church in Wilmette and took a church in Erie, Pennsylvania. I loved the church I had left and thought I'd never forget anyone's name. But the years passed, and I got very involved in the Erie church. Seldom did I reflect on the people I had left behind.

It was time for Skokie Valley to celebrate its fortieth anniversary. They called on me to be their banquet speaker on Saturday night and their worship service speaker on Sunday morning. The banquet was at a very elegant Chicagoland hotel. It was a first-class event.

I studied hard to do well. But there was one area I never thought about – reviewing all the names of the people I had served some 15 years before.

Tim Cooper was one of the students while I was there. He went on our first youth trip to Colorado. I can still picture him in the train engineer's hat he bought in Denver. I knew him well. I knew his single-parent mom very well also. Her name was Linda.

Marie and I entered the lobby of the hotel. Hors d'oeuvres and punch were abundantly available as the people mingled. Person after person came up to us. It was so great to see everyone again. But the challenge was on. Some of the names were just not there. How long could I graciously fake it?

Then Linda appeared before me with Tim. He was short as a student. He had grown into a tall, handsome man, but I still recognized him. Linda was enthusiastic. She said, "Do you remember me?"

"I sure do," I exclaimed. But my mind went blank. A few seconds seemed like an eternity. Somehow, I had to remember her name!

Suddenly her last name came to mind: *Cooper, Cooper.* I was thrilled. But what was her first name? Something from that era in the church stirred within my memory and, in a flash, it came to me. It made such sense. In all sincerity I said, "Why, you're Alice Cooper!"

Shock registered on her face, and then came laughter. I was busted. She knew I'd forgotten her name. But she was gracious as she reminded me that her name was Linda. I blushed and we laughed together.

From that moment on, I never forgot Linda - *or* Alice Cooper, for that matter. Those names will be etched on the walls of my mind until my days of senility.

58

THE NAME QUESTION

J esus was speaking about the Kingdom of God when He said, "Unless you become like a child, you shall not enter the Kingdom of Heaven." That statement is fraught with ideas about what children are like.

There are some incredible traits children have that adults have lost – like trust and innocence. They have no real possessions and a three-year-old could care less about money. Yet there are some childish traits that adults need to outgrow – like self-centeredness and uncontrolled emotions.

One Sunday, I wanted to test this "nature of a child" concept that Jesus spoke about. My sermon was on sharing our resources with others in order to meet pressing needs. Sometimes adults do well with this. Sometimes they don't. I wanted to see what children would do when one child got an abundance of something, and the other child got little.

It was all unrehearsed. No script. No warning to the children. An impromptu experience would be a good indicator of what adults might do if they became like a child.

I had pre-selected my granddaughter, Alexis Detter, to be one of the

5-year old children I would call to join me on the platform. Her mother, Rachel, was agreeable. The other 5-year old would be a volunteer from the congregation. I knew it was risky, but I was willing to take the chance.

The text spoke about generosity, even when our resources are scarce. Citing the Macedonians in II Corinthians 8, I came to the illustration part of the sermon that involved the children. What would the children do when they were given unequal portions? Would they show selfishness without compassion? Or would one empathize with the other child and share.

I called for a volunteer. A 5 year-old girl raised her hand and I beckoned her to the platform. "And what's your name?" I inquired. "My name is Megan," responded the confident little tyke. I thanked her for coming to the stage and sat her on a little chair I had placed there beforehand.

Now it was time for my granddaughter to make her appearance. I gestured in her direction and bid her come to me. She showed no signs of reticence as she stood up and walked in my direction to the stage. Most people knew she was my granddaughter and that her grandfather was giving her a little of the spotlight.

As she ascended the platform and walked towards me, I said, "And what's *your* name?" She stopped in her tracks with a major expression of shock on her face. She spoke so the whole church could hear.

"Pop Pop! Don't you know who I am?!" I could see the confusion in her eyes as she feared I was totally clueless as to who she was.

The church erupted in laughter. I put my arms around her and said, "Sure I know who you are, Alexis. I'm so glad you came up here to help Pop Pop." She settled down and I ushered her to her little chair.

Picking up a little stash of candy bars, I gave one child only one candy bar while I gave the other child five. Both faces showed bewilderment as they looked at me. "You can go back to your seats now or you can talk with each other for a second if you like."

Next thing I know, each child was holding three candy bars. It was done. With smiles on their faces, they got up and went back to their parents to the applause of the congregation.

I can't say this would work every time. But in this case, with no coaching, the children shared. It was a touching lesson in the kingdom living Jesus spoke about, with a little unexpected humor thrown in.

59

PARTING THE WATERS

As a preacher, I never quite know how the Sunday morning sermon will go. I study hard. I write my manuscript. I practice it several times. I bathe the process in prayer. I run it by Marie. But there's also the element of the unknown in the actual delivery.

Maybe the audience is responsive. Maybe they're flat. Maybe I feel energized. Maybe I feel a little foggy. Maybe I need my notes. Maybe I improvise. Maybe I make a mistake. Maybe I don't. Maybe Bill will fall sleep again. Maybe he won't. I wonder in every sermon, *What will happen?*

One Sunday, I was preaching on the power of God. I was feeling good. The audience was responsive. I was firing on all cylinders. The anointing had fallen.

Then came the illustrations about the power of God. I had a convincing string of them: *It was the power of God that created the universe! It was the power of God that brought the plagues on Egypt! It was the power of God that made the sun stand still! It was the power of God that came upon Sampson! It was the power of God that fell on Elijah's altar. It was the power of God that raised Jesus from the dead. It was the power of God that fell on the Day of Pentecost. It was the power of God that sprung Peter from jail.*

And on I went. Then it happened!

Backstory. I'm known for getting words and letters mixed up in sermons. One time I declared with great authority that all Christians should read that great Christian classic, *The Pilgrim's Progress*, by Paul Bunyan. It should have been *John* Bunyan, a Puritan from the 17th Century. Paul Bunyan is a giant lumberjack in American folklore.

Another time, I quoted a verse of *Amazing Grace* in a sermon as: *Through many dangers, snoils, and tares.* Another time it was having lunch at Roosty Tuby's (*Ruby Tuesday's*).

Back to the sermon. The illustrations about the power of God continued, *And it was the power of God that farted the Red Sea!* Instantly I knew something wrong had come out of my mouth. For a second, I wasn't sure what. But as I panned the audience, shock and bewilderment were evident on the sea of faces. It looked like the people weren't quite sure they had correctly heard what I had just said.

I think I'd have gotten through it okay, but Greg Hackenberg, one of the more outgoing teen boys sitting in the teen section to my left, exclaimed for all to hear, "Huh?!" Now the entire church was drawn to attention.

And then, like a cloudburst, the congregation erupted into robust, uncontrollable laughter, including me. My mistake had become crystal clear. There were as many tears flowing in the church as there'd be for a funeral. It took five minutes before I could continue. Even then, intermittent laughter erupted in the congregation and in me for the rest of my sermon.

In the lobby after the service, one of the older saints in the church came up to me. With a twinkle in his eye he said, "Pastor, I knew that God used wind to part the waters of the Red Sea. But I didn't know He did it *that* way. What a miracle!"

I must admit, after this I was a little shy about preaching on how God parted the Jordan River.

60

CHURCH DINNERS

ulletin bloopers usually go over well in sermons. Since this chapter is on church dinners, a few church dinner bloopers will lead the way. These are not original with me; they're anonymous although Travis Agnew, Senior Pastor of Rocky Creek Baptist Church in Greenville, South Carolina, authored some of them.

The following are reputed to have happened in real time. Even spellcheck couldn't catch these. Read carefully:

- The cost for attending the Fasting and Prayer Conference includes meals.
- Attend our ladies social. You will hear an excellent speaker and heave a healthy lunch.
- The church will host an evening of fine dining, super entertainment, and gracious hostility.
- Potluck supper Sunday at 5:00 PM – prayer and medication to follow.
- The Ladies Bible Study will be held Thursday morning at 10 a.m. All ladies are invited to lunch in the Fellowship Hall after the B.S. is done.

- The pastor would appreciate it if the ladies of the congregation would lend him their electric girdles for the pancake breakfast next Sunday.
- The Men's Bar-B-Q is this Saturday. We're collecting hot dogs, buns, and porn and beans.
- Please sign up to help with the meals for our home-bound next Sunday night. Eleven sinners need to be delivered.
- The Community Lenten Lunches are every Tuesday at noon at the Community Center. They are run by the Area Minstrel Association.
- Next Sunday is the family hayride and bonfire at the Fowlers. Beverages and desserts provided. Bring your own hot dogs and guns.
- Our monthly potluck dinner will be hell this Wednesday night.

The tradition of eating at religious gatherings goes back to the festivals of the Jews in the Old Testament and to the love feasts of the church in the New Testament. Meals have been part of the faith community's experience for millennia.

But church dinners aren't as common as they used to be. With the advent of the megachurch and the speed of life, church dinners and potlucks seem to be a dying event. Even smaller churches are having a hard time keeping them on their schedules.

I grew up with church potluck dinners and picnics. People brought a dish to share. A-M would bring a main dish and N-Z a salad or dessert. There was always plenty to eat.

You'd never quite know how things would taste. No one made lasagna the same. The potato salad was creamy or pasty. The deviled eggs were bland or filled with little crunchies. The scalloped potatoes were creamy or milky, some with browned mushroom soup on top and some loaded with crunchy onions. Sometimes the potatoes weren't thoroughly cooked. The baked beans were never the same. Regardless, no one mentioned the taste disparities even if there was a bad dish "elephant in the room." It was just part of the tradition.

I had never heard of tureen dinners until we moved to Grace Church in Erie, Pennsylvania. The church was smaller in those days with opportunities for many all-church food functions: a smorgasbord at Christmas, a church picnic in the summer, 'souper' suppers in the winter, and Wednesday night tureen dinners during the school year. I soon learned that a tureen dish was the same as a casserole at a potluck dinner. I simply added a new word to my vocabulary, but I'd been supping at dinners like this all my life.

The tureen dinners were quite popular, and they became a portal for new people coming into the church. They'd come Sunday morning and be invited to the tureen dinner on Wednesday night. They'd often come and enjoy the fellowship.

One cold, snowy February night during those days, Marie and I decided to check out the RV show at the mall. We needed some "summer" at that time of the year. As we were walking down the main concourse, we happened to see a couple new to our church. They stopped and engaged us in conversation, telling us they were new to the area and thrilled to have found such a welcoming church family.

Then with bright eyes and a big smile of satisfaction, the lady said, "We especially love those Wednesday night *latrine* dinners."

Latrine dinners!

That was it for us. Laughter erupted from within, but we had to control it until we could remove ourselves from their presence – which we managed to do quickly. We found our way into the nearest motor home and fell on the sofa, out of control with laughter.

A latrine dinner! All kinds of images entered our minds. Had I been older, I might have politely corrected her mistake. But I couldn't bring myself to tell her how far afield her word selection had been.

After that, whenever we'd see this dear couple at the weekly dinners, they'd smile and we'd talk. But she never spoke of the dinners by name again to me. I had to wonder – when did she find out that they were *tureen* dinners?

61

THE DINNER ROLLS

Grandma Harding, as she was known to everyone at Grace Church, still lived alone in a modest little farmhouse where she died suddenly on her 90th birthday. She had been getting ready to go out for a birthday lunch with her son.

She's been gone for years now, but she's not forgotten by any of us who knew her. Her trademark, hearty "Amen!" could be heard multiple times during sermons and at the end of songs. Sometimes she "Amen-ed" at awkward times – like at a key pause in a cantata when she thought it was over.

Grandma Harding was also known for her flatulence. She'd go putt-putting down the aisle toward her regular seat while my kids giggled themselves half silly. Not just my kids – but half the church.

And talk about a prayer warrior! She had no rival in the church. She attended every prayer meeting, praying with great fervor, her requests often bathed in tears.

She was equally known for her cooking and baking, especially her dinner rolls. No church dinner was complete without Grandma Harding's rolls: hard on the outside, soft in the middle and brushed with a sweet butter sauce. Everyone raved about her rolls. And so did I.

Until one night she had our whole family over for dinner.

The six of us and Grandma Harding sat around the table, with her old iron stove in the background. She knew exactly how much wood she needed and how to fire it up to a certain temperature. Pies, rolls, roasts, turkeys – she cooked them all in that old stove.

During our dinner, she volunteered that one time she was cooking and found a mouse in the kitchen trap.

"I just put it in the stove fire," she said with a tone of proud accomplishment. Marie and I just glanced at each other. We weren't sure that information did a lot for our appetites.

Halfway through my meal, I realized I hadn't eaten my dinner roll yet. "Please pass the butter," I requested, as I broke open my roll.

Marie saw it first.

Sitting inside one half of the roll were two of the largest, black carpenter ants I had ever seen. Half of their bodies were protruding from the roll with their two antennae sticking straight up.

They were dead, of course, but I thought *I* was about to die. What was I to do? I couldn't say anything or I'd embarrass Grandma Harding. If I showed my kids, they'd die laughing. And Marie? She was watching me the whole time. There was sympathy in her eyes and a grin on her face.

You've got to think of this as a missionary experience, I coached myself. Over the years, I've traveled to many foreign countries where I've faced awkward food situations more challenging than this one.

With sleight of hand, I pinched off the area of the roll occupied by the ants, placed it gently under my plate, loaded the rest of the roll with butter, and made short work of it.

Even though the butter made the roll easier to swallow, the mental image of those ants was impossible to dislodge. I labored over every bite of food for the rest of the meal. The other half of the roll was almost impossible to eat.

Then came the feared question. Grandma said, "I know how you love my rolls. How about another one?"

I graciously declined and she didn't insist. Whew!

From that moment on, Grandma Harding's rolls were on probation. When our kids retreated to the car, I told them what had happened. They responded, "Only you, Dad!" and giggled themselves half to death. I told them I'd give Grandma's rolls one more try at the next church dinner.

The inevitable next church dinner arrived and, sure enough, Grandma Harding's rolls were on the buffet line. I could hear the people around me raving about them.

Okay, I'll give them one more chance, I thought as I picked up a roll.

I took my seat at the table with my family and broke open my roll. Déjà vu. No ants this time, but one lone strand of Grandma's hair held the two halves together. I once heard Grandma tell Marie that she only washed her hair once a month.

Right there, the probation period ended. I never ate another one of Grandma Harding's rolls.

At later church dinners, people continued to rave about the rolls. I'd think to myself, *If only they knew.* But I never wanted to dampen the party spirit by divulging secrets.

It wouldn't surprise me if Grandma Harding is baking her rolls in Heaven as a new kind of manna. I'm sure the heavenly hosts would be raving. Even *I* would eat one of her rolls at a Heavenly banquet.

Maybe that's why I like the old hymn, "When the Roll is Called Up Yonder, I'll Be There."

215

62

THE BULLETIN BLOOPER

In language, is there anything worse than *verbal* blunders? Why yes, there is. It's when blunders appear in print. You may be able to waffle on whether you actually mispronounced something and even be able to sow some doubt in the minds of others. But when a blunder or blooper appears in black-and-white, there's no getting around it or denying it.

Church bulletin bloopers have been a hit for years. There are many classics. Some of them are always funny: *Bertha Belch, a missionary from Africa, will be speaking at Calvary Methodist next Sunday. Come hear Bertha Belch all the way from Africa.*

Some of them are overused: *The Low Self-Esteem Support Group will meet on Thursday from 7:00 to 8:30pm. Please use the back door.*

Some of them are a little edgy: *Tuesday at 4:00pm will be a homemade ice cream social. All ladies giving milk will please come early.*

But if you're looking for fresh material to add to the list, the best place to look is probably within your own church bulletin. Like the night of one of our church's Annual Meeting. The bulletin said, *The meeting tonight will be conducted in accordance with Robber's Rules of Order.*

But there's a better one.

Some years ago, I preached a sermon series on spiritual gifts, those special God-given capacities the Holy Spirit gives to Christians. These gifts make it possible to minister effectively and specifically to others so they can grow spiritually.

In the first week of the series, I explained the various spiritual gifts from the major New Testament passages. I created a bulletin insert listing the various gifts with definitions.

In the second sermon, I talked about how to recognize one's spiritual gifts. Once again, I created a bulletin insert about the gifts. This time, it was a tool for people to assess themselves and check which spiritual gift or gifts they thought they might have. It was a special time of discovery for many.

Now to the very practical. In the third and last sermon, I spoke about what kinds of things a person might do if they had certain spiritual gifts. I created a list of about forty relevant, modern-day possibilities. Once again, it found its way into the bulletin as an insert. I told the church to look over the many options and consider the ones that captured their interest the most. They were to check their top choices and return them the next week. We'd then work with them to find the ministries that most closely aligned with their spiritual gifts.

I was getting ready to go to our church family camp during the week leading up to this final sermon. I didn't get all the usual administrative things accomplished like proof-reading the bulletin.

But not to worry. I had an excellent secretary, Lois Nelson. She was on top of quality control – unless too much work was coming at her. Such was the case that week. When the Senior Pastor was extra busy, so was Lois. But I never gave it a second thought.

The sermon went well that Sunday. I closed the service and quickly headed home to grab a quick lunch with my family. Soon all of us would be off to Camp Burton.

A number of families from the church were also registered for camp.

I got there a little early to get things in order, as I was to be the speaker for the Moms and Dads that week. The other families would roll in later.

Soon afterward, the families began to arrive. Dave Winn could hardly wait to find me. "Where's Al? Where's Al?" he queried around camp. He finally found me.

I saw him coming. His gait was swift. He had a crescent-moon grin. His eyes sparkled mischievously like stars. I knew him well enough to know that something interesting was about to happen.

"I want you to see the ministry I'm signing up for on this insert." He continued, "I'm not the only one signing up for this. There are a whole bunch more. Take a look!" He was so eager to show me the insert.

I couldn't believe what I saw. I felt instantly sheepish, but there it was in black and white, one of the best bulletin bloopers I'd ever seen. I thought to myself, *Why couldn't a mistake have been made on some other word?*

Three quarters of the way into the list, the ministry opportunity was supposed to say *Pantry Ministry*. Instead, it said *Panty Ministry*.

Lois and I took an incredible ribbing over this. And the church laughed about it for weeks. The *pantry* ministry did great. But oddly enough, the *panty* ministry never got off the ground. By common consensus, it was agreed that there were no spiritual gifts connected to a panty ministry, unless the Apostle Paul forgot to include it and we were the first to discover it.

The outcome? There were no free panties at our church. Ladies still had to purchase them in the women's section of the department stores. And Dave had to find another ministry.

63

THE HAIR

Part of my reputation is that I'm known as the "Coupon Man." I collect coupons. When we go out to eat or shop, we save money. If I don't have a coupon for a certain place, I wait for a special. Bottom line – bargains attract me.

Our community was known for their Lenten Lunches. On the six Thursdays during Lent, the clergy of West Millcreek would choose a church in which to hold a service followed by a lunch. Pastors from different area churches took turns bringing the message each week, but only one church would host the event for the duration of Lent.

Not only were these services inspirational, the lunch was cheap. Only $2 per person. A bargain, indeed!

One Thursday morning, I announced to my two secretaries that I'd be treating them to lunch – the Lenten Lunch. I knew they thought I was being somewhat cheap. But at the same time, they enjoyed being with people in the community.

Our church had gone through some difficulties, and we lost quite a few members to a church a few miles from us.

That week, the lunch crew was from the church to which a number of our people had migrated. Some of the people who left our church were on the serving teams that day. The teams brought the lunches to the tables, so I'd be certain to see some former members.

Annie Watson, Kathy Herrmann, and I finally found a table in the crowd of 200 people. At the table sat the three of us, three pastors, and two others. One of the pastors was from the church to which our people had gone. We did our best to pretend that it wasn't a little awkward.

Soon the meals were served and yes, our table was served by people who had left our church. Everyone smiled politely.

It was a soup and sandwich lunch. I can't remember what kind of soup we had but I'll always remember the chicken salad croissant sandwich. It only took one bite for me to realize that the sandwich was a hit. I took a second bite, and then a third.

Suddenly something didn't seem right. I swallowed but something pulled on my tongue. It dawned on me – it was a hair.

I didn't want anyone to know my plight, so I discreetly tried to move my tongue to free it from the hair. No luck. I put my hand over my mouth with a napkin like I was wiping it as I reached in with a finger to dislodge the hair. Still no luck.

I knew I was in trouble because my gag reflex was about to kick in. I had to do something. I hoped no one would see. With as little fanfare as possible, I reached inside my mouth and with my right-hand thumb and index finger, I was able to grab the hair. I began to pull on it.

As I pulled on the hair, I felt movement in my throat. I realized it was a long hair. The only question was, "How long?" I pulled on it with my right hand as far as I could without it becoming totally obvious. But the hair was longer than my pull. It was the left hand to the rescue. I continued to pull on the hair as it ascended my throat.

The hair had tiny little bits of food on it as it made its way out of my mouth. I was mortified. I quickly looked around the table. It was silent and all eyes were on me. I wanted to crawl into a hole.

My secretaries were sitting directly to my left. They saw the whole thing. Instead of ignoring my plight and making nothing of it, with no compassion at all they erupted into laughter that shook their chairs. I was thinking, *Shut up, please!* but they couldn't stop.

And the three pastors? They looked at me soberly and straight-faced, never cracking a smile, including the pastor of our former members who served our table.

I couldn't finish my sandwich, and soon we were out the door. My secretaries couldn't stop laughing. "Only you!" they chuckled, because I often have strange food things happen to me. "What are the odds of *you* getting that hair, and with our former members and their pastor to witness it?"

We returned to the office and for the rest of the afternoon, those two ladies replayed the hair extrication scene in their minds over and over to recurrent waves of laughter.

That night, Annie graphically told her husband the story. Mike laughed, but not nearly as hard. Eventually bedtime came and they reclined. But Annie couldn't get the reruns out of her mind. Every time she thought of the hair scene, she laughed until she shook the bed.

After about half an hour of repeated bed-shaking, Mike said, "You've got to stop that laughing so we can get to sleep!" The next morning when I came to work, I was greeted by two giggling secretaries.

This happened years ago. But if you'd ask them about the incident, they'd laugh almost as hard as they did that day. And they'd tell you that it ranks as one of their all-time funniest memories.

Secretaries' postscript:

I sent the above chapter to my two secretaries for their reading pleasure. Below are their responses.

Kathy – Oh, Al. You are correct. That was one of the funniest stories of my LIFE! Annie and I were like 7th grade girls with our uncontrollable laughter. I've often wondered if it would have been as funny if "that church" hadn't been the ones preparing the lunch?!

Annie – "Al, I started smiling with remembrance from the first word. By the time I finished, it all came flooding back to me and I laughed all over again. It's a story for the ages! I'll never forget that day. It wouldn't have been half as funny if it happened to anyone else. Especially having those stone-sober pastors at our table. At least we know how to have a good time!! Sorry if it was at your expense. Still laughing!"

64

THE ALLERGY

Sometimes I get my facts mixed up. And sometimes it can be embarrassing.

We had a great worship band at Grace Church in Erie, Pennsylvania. Not only did they play well, they were friends who liked to be together. You see, ministry isn't just about doing tasks together, it's about close relationships. And that bled through in the ethos that came across to the congregation from the platform.

It was only natural, then, that Marie and I had the band over to our house for a picnic. We wanted them to have a good time just being together around some picnic food. We provided the groceries. All they had to do was show up.

Members of the band began to arrive. They were enjoying themselves on our deck with plenty of conversation, laughter, reminiscing, and dreaming about the future. The cars lined the street and filled our driveway.

Everyone had arrived except Mike and Nancy Clark. Mike played the guitar and Nancy sang in the band. The two of them frequently did duets. Much of their music, they wrote.

I went to greet them as they got out of their car. After a few welcoming hugs, I noticed that Nancy was holding several containers of food. "You didn't have to bring anything. It's all provided."

"I know," she replied. "But I'm on a special diet. I have a yeast allergy, so I brought my own food."

"Oh," I replied. "I've known you all these years, and I never knew that."

I ushered them onto the deck. She set her food containers down in a secluded place, so no one would mistakenly eat her special food.

After a prayer of grace, we dove into the meal. I observed Nancy eating her food. She seemed to enjoy it but, in my eyes, it was nothing compared to the hot dogs, hamburgers, baked beans, deviled eggs, potato salad, and potato chips on the table.

Before long, we were done with the main meal and into the desserts. Nancy had brought her own little dessert as well. As we enjoyed the sweets, everyone was involved in lively and enjoyable conversation.

I reflected on Nancy's restricted diet. She had other physical problems as well – problems that caused her significant pain, the result of excessive scar tissue from multiple surgeries. I was thinking, *Pain and a restricted diet? I feel bad for Nancy.*

I retreated to my initial conversation with her when she got out of the car with her food and a question came to my mind. Quite coincidentally, the buzz of conversation on the deck stopped at the very moment I asked Nancy my question.

"So tell me, Nancy. How long have you had your yeast infection?"

Everyone heard my question and there was an immediate explosion of uncontrollable laughter. It wouldn't stop. Nancy couldn't stop laughing and neither could her husband. I was confident that the neighbors were curious about what was happening on our deck. I was hoping they didn't think we all had "one too many."

For a second, I had no idea what I had said. What had precipitated this outburst of laughter? Marie jumped in, "Do you know what you said?"

"Yes," came my reply. "I wanted to know how long Nancy has had her yeast infection."

"Al," she replied, "it's a yeast *allergy*, not a yeast infection."

Suddenly I felt heat flash though my body as I blushed. The group laughed even harder. How could I make such a mistake? Mike said with a twinkle in his eye, "You're getting a little personal with my wife, aren't you?" The waves of laughter continued off and on for about twenty minutes.

Believe me, I'll never get a yeast allergy and a yeast infection mixed up again. The band will never let me forget it, either. And you can almost hear the reverberation of laughter in my neighborhood till this day.

65

MY NEIGHBOR

J esus told us that the two greatest commandments are to love God completely and to love our neighbor as ourselves. Most of us have room to improve in both departments, but let's zero in on the neighbor part.

Our neighbor isn't just confined to those who live around us. Jesus went so far as to put even strangers into the neighbor category. In fact, everyone who crosses our path in any given day is our neighbor. They are there by divine appointment.

But sometimes God needs to remind me.

Marie and I took a much-needed trip to Hilton Head some years ago. At the airport, we checked the flight schedules on the monitor and all was well. But for some reason, we were delayed out of Erie. In the best of circumstances, it was going to be a tight connection in Pittsburgh.

When we arrived late in Pittsburgh, we found that our connecting gate to Savannah was on another concourse. There seemed to be no human way to make the connection, but we still wanted to try.

We took off running with our unwieldy carry-ons. The clock was running faster than we were. Our lungs were screaming with pain. And sweating profusely, we were out of breath. But the gate was finally in sight. We got there with two minutes to spare. Hallelujah! The plane was still at the gate.

Just as we arrived, we saw the agent shut the gate door. She wouldn't let us board.

I had read Herb Cohen's book, *You Can Negotiate Anything* some years back. And I heard leadership guru John Maxwell, in person, talk about how he negotiated getting on a golf course in Scotland when it should have been impossible. Now it was my turn.

I explained the situation to the attendant and appealed to board the plane. I got nowhere. I tried all the negotiating skills I knew but nothing worked. Five minutes into negotiations, the plane was still sitting there.

I had one more option – ask for the supervisor. At least *that* was successful.

Soon she appeared at the gate. I made my appeals, which soon turned into demands. She resolutely refused. She was a stranger to me, so I got as nasty as I could without sinning in word or deed. The last thing on my mind was humor.

She kept her composure and asked for my ticket. I handed it to her and she read it out loud to me. "REV. Al Detter."

Only my title was in capital letters on my ticket.

She gave me a look. So did Marie, as she backed away from me. After calmly booking us on the next flight, the supervisor returned my ticket as she said, "Here you are, *reverend*." Through all this, the plane sat by the gate like icing on a ruined cake. Finally, it departed, and we grabbed some lunch. Following the incident, I could tell Marie was anything but proud of her preacher husband.

After we boarded the next flight, I sat there brooding like Jonah when the Spirit of God said to me, *You didn't know that lady but she was a neighbor to you. Did you bless her? Did you bring Me glory? Especially with the large letters REV as she handled your ticket?*

I was smitten in my spirit. I probably ruined her day and the reputation of the clergy. What if I had smiled through all the frustration instead?

Right there on that plane I said to the Lord, "Please forgive me! I was a jerk. If you can put me in contact with that lady when we return to Pittsburgh next week, I'll apologize."

It was an impossible request. But every day for the entire week I prayed, *Lord, if you could arrange for me to see that lady again, I'll make things right.* I knew the magnitude of the request given the size of the airport.

As we boarded our return flight in Savannah, I prayed that I'd see that supervisor again. I prayed all the way to Pittsburgh. I knew I'd recognize her; I hadn't forgotten her uncooperative face. We landed in Pittsburgh and had to go through the ticket counter, seemingly miles from the gate of incident. I thought, *Not a chance of seeing that lady again.*

Marie and I were standing in the long line. Perhaps nine ticket counters were open. I continued to pray, *Lord, are we still on? Will you get me to that lady?*

At that moment, I spotted her behind one of the ticket counters! Now I was praying, *Lord, get me to her counter!*

Finally, it was our turn. Incredibly, we were directed to her counter. Sheepishly, but with a spring in my step, I stood before her. She took my ticket, and had yet to look up when I said, "Do you remember me?"

She lifted her head and the light dawned on her with a look that expressed, *Not you again, REV!*

She said, "How could I forget?"

Before she said another word, I contritely and sincerely apologized. She accepted it and my burden lifted as her countenance brightened. Then tears welled up in her eyes as she said, "I've been at this job for over twenty years. I've encountered a host of nasty people over those years. But you're the only one who's ever apologized. Thanks, REV." And then she smiled.

Marie and I couldn't believe we had encountered that supervisor again! It was a miracle. All three of us parted with a smile and chuckle of satisfaction. In God's great mercy, He had given me a chance to make things right with my neighbor. And I think God was smiling.

66

AN APRIL FOOL

April Fools' Day is a pranks and practical jokes day each April 1 in the United States. Once the victim takes the bait, the jokester exposes the prank with a resounding, "April Fools!"

The origin of this ignoble day is up for grabs. If you do some research, there's no clear path to its starting point. But one thing is sure. Whatever its origin, it plays to the heart of the human soul – most people like to tease. April Fools Day is here to stay.

Years ago, widespread pranks were staged from media outlets like newspapers, radio, and TV stations. But people are jumpy these days. Causing a public panic or a rush of calls on cell phones or crashing the Internet runs the risk of danger and litigation. So pranks on wide-scale audiences are less likely.

But that doesn't stop individuals at home, school, work, and play from celebrating a good April Fools' "gotcha." I've been practicing it all my life. So have many of my friends. For the prankster, this Scripture verse might apply: *It is more blessed to give than to receive.*

Please note that I didn't mention "church" in the paragraph above. I mean, who'd imagine that April Fools jokes could happen at church. Isn't that a place where truth and honesty always triumph over falsehood and deception?

You'd think that you could trust colleagues on a church staff *every day* of the year. Aren't trust and believability components that propel collegiality and ministry forward? When one of them says or does something, you believe them. Including when you have a complete mental lapse that it's April 1.

I've been hosting tours to Israel since 1984. During those years, I developed a close friendship with my guide, Malcolm Cartier. We have mutual appreciation and respect.

In 2004, terrorism had dried up tourism in the Holy Land, so Malcolm brought the Holy Land to the States. It was a two-day virtual tour of Israel, complete with a Saturday morning full Israeli breakfast. It was the closest thing to taking an international tour without leaving town.

Malcolm had a continuing itinerary in the States with many churches and he'd fly back and forth from Israel. On one trip, he had been detained in London because of a passport situation.

Shortly thereafter, my secretary handed me a letter. It was on official State Department letterhead informing me that the unimaginable had happened. Malcolm had been arrested and detained in London because he was running a money-laundering operation for terrorist insurgents. The honoraria that he had been getting from the American churches went directly to the rebel cause.

Tears welled up and I felt an indescribable clench in the pit in my stomach. I thought I had entered the realm of the unthinkable. In my distraught condition I read on.

"Because Malcolm was at your church, you and members of your staff and church will be subject to federal interviews. No one is above suspicion."

I finished the letter in shock. Burning heat flushed through me. A mental picture of Malcolm was front and center in my mind. I couldn't fathom such betrayal from a long-term, trusted friend. I knew I was done for the day.

Bolting out of my office, I rushed past my secretary sitting at her desk. "What's wrong?" she inquired.

I retorted, "I don't want to talk about it. I'm gone for the day," and turned left to go out the door to the parking lot.

That's when my associate, Pastor Mike Watson, found me. With a grin on his face, he said, "April Fools!" I glared at him with fire in my eyes, "Well, I don't think this is one bit funny," and I continued my flight out the door.

I got into my driver's seat and looked to my left. There in the copy-center window was my entire staff peering at me with a mixture of mirth and puzzlement. *How could I be upset now that I knew it was a practical joke?*

I had been so shocked that my body was trembling, and my spirit was shaken. I had to leave to regain my wits. I was gone for several hours before I could return.

While gone, I relived repeatedly the shocking impact of reading the letter. Why didn't I see through it? But the letterhead looked so authentic. The text sounded so official. The circumstances were of such a nature that, even though inconceivable, they could have lined up with actual facts.

I returned to the office and called my staff together so we could decompress. They told me how they pulled it off. I apologized for overreacting. "I still don't think it was funny," I objected. But they all responded in chorus, "Oh yes it was!"

I managed a smile and all was well once again, especially since I knew that Malcolm was truly innocent.

You can probably see how this April Fools prank lives in infamy. Many pranks have been pulled on me over the years, but this one surpasses them all.

67

THE BOOT

It was a cold and snowy January night. A family in our church had invited us over for dinner. The six in our family and the five in theirs gathered around the table. Rhoda outdid herself on the meal.

After dinner, all the kids ran off to their respective rooms for a night of fun. The adults went downstairs to the family room. A cozy fire in the fireplace set a good mood for fellowship.

Rhoda McIntire was a very colorful personality. She wasn't bashful about anything. Like the night she and her sister came up to me after the New Year's Eve service with a spray can in hand. "Pastor," she said, "This is a special formula for balding hair. It will grow your hair back immediately. May I have permission to spray your balding spot?" I sensed that she was really trying to minister to her pastor.

I gave her permission. She sprayed. The thinning hairs thickened. My balding scalp turned hair-color brown. She felt satisfied. Need I say that my hair is still thinning?

With that as "color commentary," you can imagine that there was no lack of lively conversation and laughter among us that night. Her husband, Jack, was the quiet type. He was glad Rhoda held the spotlight.

As the evening wore on, the front doorbell sounded. It was a teenage friend of our hosts' daughter, Renee. She wanted to hang out for a while.

A tray for shoes and boots lay at the bottom of the stairs and the teenage guest added her boots to the wintry collection.

Enjoyable conversation flowed among the adults. The kids were enjoying themselves replete with the usual sounds of kids squealing, laughing, running, and interruptions for Mom and Dad. Everyone was having a good time.

Little 3-year-old Joey was in the middle of being potty-trained. At one point, he got between us adults and appealed to his mother, "I have to pee." Rhoda deflected him and continued to chat. He ran off.

A few minutes went by before Joey marched in again. With a little more urgency he announced, "I've got to pee!"

"Hold it a little longer, and mommy will be right with you," came the response. Off the little tyke ran again. I'm wondering, *Rhoda! What are you thinking? Take the kid to the potty!* But I didn't want to interfere.

A third time, the little guy burst upon us to make his appeal, "Mommy, I really have to pee!"

"I'll be with you in just a sec," came the reassuring reply, and on she went with her story. Joey ran away. Finally, Rhoda got up to assist him, but Joey was nowhere in sight. So Rhoda went exploring when she came upon a very unexpected sight.

There was little Joey, standing tall and proud...peeing into the boot of the neighbor girl.

"Joey!" exclaimed Rhoda, "You can't do that!"

"That's okay, Mommy," came the reply. "I don't have to go now. Can I go play?"

Rhoda was next to speechless, a rare moment indeed. Marie and I were laughing so hard we almost peed our pants.

The pee in the boot presented a real problem for Rhoda. What would she tell her daughter's friend? I mean, there was no avoiding reality. How could the girl go home in the snowy cold with a pee-soaked boot?

Eventually, Renee and her friend returned to the family room. Rhoda gathered them by the shoe tray.

"Well," managed Rhoda, "Joey had to go to the bathroom, and he peed in your boot." (Rhoda neglected to include the part about Joey's many unanswered requests for help leading up to the "accident.")

"He what?!" shrieked the owner of the boots. "You're kidding me!"

Rhoda had a tough time explaining this most unusual situation. It wasn't long until the girl realized that, indeed, her boot was wet, and it wasn't melted snow.

"I'll wash it out and put the hairdryer on it," volunteered Rhoda. The girl resolutely declined the offer. There was no convincing her that she might ever be able to wear that boot again.

Rhoda loaned the girl some boots to go home, along with a promise to buy her new ones as soon as possible. The pee-flooded boots found their way to the trash.

The next time little Joey said he had to pee, there was immediate action!

68

THE RESORT

Seven Springs Resort, nestled in the rolling hills of southwestern Pennsylvania, is a perfect place for a retreat. And so it was that I rolled into the resort on a Monday afternoon for our district's pastors and wives gathering. The only problem? Marie couldn't attend with me.

The schedule called for a Monday evening dinner and ran through an afternoon session on Wednesday.

I checked in at the front desk, got my keys, and headed to find my accommodations.

The retreat organizers provided a roommate for me because his wife wasn't with him, either. My roommate had already arrived, so we introduced ourselves. Even though we had never met, we became fast friends.

But we had one minor disagreement. The accommodations included a king-size bed and a sleeper sofa. I've had some bad experiences with sleepers, but I offered the bed to him. He insisted on the sleeper. He wanted to defer to "an older brother in the Lord."

We went back and forth until I finally said, "Okay. I'll agree to take the king-size bed under one condition. I'll take it tonight if we can make a trade tomorrow night. You get the bed and I get the sleeper." Agreed. Soon we were off to dinner.

In the morning, I received a message to return home. It was nothing urgent, but something needed my attention. For sure, my new roommate would now get the big bed.

After some excellent sessions in the morning and lunch, it was time for me to head home. I had already vacated my room and my bags were in my car, but I had not yet surrendered the keys.

Wouldn't you know it? I had a compelling need to use the bathroom. With no idea where a public bathroom was in the resort, I devised a plan. I still have a key and I'm close to my former room. I'll use *that* bathroom. As our group made their way to the afternoon sessions, I made my way back to the room.

Entering, I made a beeline for the bathroom. I didn't shut the bathroom door because it was urgent, and I was alone. Soon I discovered that it was going to be a bit lengthier process than I had anticipated. So I began to sing. I mean, sing robustly out loud. And what better songs to sing than the worship songs we had just been singing at the retreat?

I'm singing away and conclude my business. I leave the bathroom and walk down the short hallway toward the little living room, where the front door was located.

Still singing, I was suddenly stunned. Sitting primly on the sofa were two total strangers, a man and a woman. They were waiting for whoever was about to appear from the hallway. A hot rush of embarrassment flooded through me. Bathroom business and singing are very personal. They had heard it all.

"What in heaven's name are you doing in our suite, let alone our bathroom!?" spoke a stern and threatening voice. "How did you get in here?" I could tell they were guests who had nothing to do with our retreat. I felt like Goldilocks when the three bears came home and found her in Baby Bear's bed.

I regained my composure and blurted out, "What are **you** doing here? This is **my** suite!"

"No," the man retorted, "this is **our** suite! We just got the keys from the front desk." He dangled them in plain sight. This was suddenly becoming a jigsaw puzzle in which the pieces were not fitting together well.

I dangled my key in return. They stared at me and I stared at them. It was a momentary impasse the awkward likes of which I'd never before experienced.

"There must be some explanation," I finally said in a more soothing manner. "Let me call the front desk." They were still piercing me with suspicious looks, but they had simmered down some.

"Hi. This is Al in Room 19. Two people are in this room claiming that it's theirs. Do you have any idea how this might have happened?" There was a pregnant pause.

"I think I can explain," came the reply. "Your roommate said you were leaving today so we moved him to a smaller room to accommodate the couple that's currently in your room. We thought you were long gone."

Suddenly, I understood. I explained the situation to the couple and finally their *we've been invaded* look subsided. Embarrassment still shrouded me as we all chuckled, shook hands, and parted ways.

From that day forward, whenever I'm in a hotel or at a resort and the bathroom beckons me, even if I'm certain it's my room, I engage the entry deadbolt and shut the bathroom door.

I can sing with more freedom that way!

69

THE COUNTERFEIT LETTER

Did you ever wonder how long outward shows of affection should happen in marriages?

Marie and I went out for dinner with a pillar couple in our church. They were in the front seat and we in the back. We were married ten years, they twenty-five.

I held Marie's hand and pecked her on the cheek. Jim caught that scene in his rear view mirror and remarked, "Don't get frisky in the back seat." To which I replied, "Why don't you hold hands in the front seat?"

I'll never forget his words, "When you're married as long as we, you don't need to kiss and hold hands." His wife agreed. Marie and I looked at each other stunned. He was an NFL football fan, and I said, "Maybe that play ought to be up for review."

That's not true for Scott and Miriam Crossman. They've been married for nearly fifty years. You'd think they were newlyweds. Scott holds her hand in public. He pays attention to her. He buys her nice and thoughtful gifts for special occasions like her birthday, anniversary, and Christmas.

Each year they fly to a resort in Mexico. It's another honeymoon.

Scott gets on Facebook on the anniversary of meeting each other, their engagement, and their wedding and he tells the total of days since then for each one. Sometimes the total hours. He's an accountant.

And Miriam? She drinks it in. You can tell that she's his lady and he's her man. There's nothing flashy, nothing showy, nothing gushy. Just a mature way of being together in a natural romantic connection that's rarely seen. I'd put this couple in the top three of all the couples I've known for marital satisfaction and manifested love.

It wasn't a surprise then when Scott found me with a letter.

Backstory. Our church used to hold yearly men's retreats. One year, the retreat was on marriage. We must have had forty men – some single, some in marital difficulty, and some doing well. What were the odds that Scott would be there? After all, he probably had the best marriage of anyone.

But he was there. He loves marital enrichment. He loves seminars on marriage. He and Miriam have taught classes on marriage to engaged couples for years. Of course, he likes the fun and fellowship that the guys on retreat have, too. But this marriage retreat really drew him in. End of backstory.

Friday night's kick-off session started with good, robust singing led by worship leaders with guitars. A challenging message on marriage hit home. A couple of good sessions on marriage captivated the guys on Saturday morning.

Then came the lunch break.

Scott found me in the mess hall standing in the food line. He handed me a letter. "Would you read this to the guys at the 2 o'clock session?"

"What is it?" I inquired. "It's a letter by Miriam. She'd like you to read it to the guys." And then he added this line, "I haven't read it. She wants *me* to hear it when you read it to the men."

"Do you mind if I read it first?" I responded. "I think that will work," he said. I took the letter and he departed.

After lunch, I read the letter. It was amazing. Miriam was singing Scott's praises like I'd never heard before. Everything was in superlatives. How thoughtful he was. How handsome he was. How creative he was. How he was the man of her dreams. And on and on. I thought, *Scott's going to love this, or he's going to be a little embarrassed.* But reading the letter was his request and I'd oblige.

We have a culture of transparency in our church. It's not unusual for people to get before our congregation and share their journeys. Sometimes they talk about a knothole in their lives and how they got through it. Sometimes they're *in* a storm and the church can be there for them. So it wasn't unusual for me to ask someone to share their difficult journey. I asked John to start the 2 o'clock session. I told Scott that I'd read his letter after John shared his story.

John was a broken man. His wife had cheated on him and left him. He told his story with tears and sobs. The men were drawn in. There wasn't a dry eye in the place. When John was finished, we circled around him, laid hands on him, and fervently prayed for the situation.

As the men retreated to their seats, I went to the podium. I pulled out the letter and prepared to read it when suddenly Scott darted out of his seat. In a flash, he was by my side. He stripped the letter from my hand and whispered, "You can't read this!" He could see my bewilderment and reiterated, "Trust me! You can't read this!" It wasn't the time to have a conversation, so I deferred and introduced the speaker.

As soon as the session was over, I went to Scott and said, "What's the deal?" He came clean. "Miriam didn't write that letter. *I did.* It was supposed to be funny. The guys would be drawn in and then be told that they'd been had. I couldn't let that happen. Not after John!"

Yes, it was quite comical. The joke was known only by the four of us – Scott, Miriam, Marie, and me. But in this I rejoice; on occasion Marie has written letters to me like Scott wrote about himself. Except they've been only for my eyes, and I didn't write them.

70

THE PINK SHIRT

For starters, I'm colorblind. I can see certain basic colors, but reds and greens can be a problem. Red letters disappear on black backgrounds. Red flowers disappear among green leaves. Shades of color are impossible. I've never seen purple; it's blue to me. I can wear pink and never know it.

Gannon University is nestled in downtown Erie, Pennsylvania. Some years ago, they had a championship-contending women's basketball team under the able coaching of Cleve Wright. Cleve was also an Elder in my church.

During that period, I was an adjunct Speech Professor at Gannon. It was Speech 101 and it was a required course. Mostly freshmen were enrolled, but there was a smattering of students – sophomores through seniors – who waited to take the course.

From time to time, some of the Gannon athletes turned up in my classes: football players, Lacrosse players, baseball players, wrestlers, and basketball players. I wanted my students to know I cared about them so I showed up at their athletic contests whenever I could.

One semester, several of the women's basketball team members were in my class. They were a contender that season and exciting to watch.

I made it a priority to go to as many games as possible. Then I'd talk about the game with the players at the next class.

Every February, the university opened its doors for free at one of their basketball games. The reason? They were promoting a cause – fundraising for breast cancer research and treatment. That meant a pink T-shirt with the black ribbon logo on it would be available. I'd buy a shirt for a worthy cause and get into the game for free. An excellent deal.

Tables were set up in the lobby. Teams were selling T-shirts and other fundraising merchandise. Just the pink shirt was sufficient for me. I bought one.

Of course, the expectation was to wear it at the game, so I donned the shirt and walked into the arena. The stands were filled with pink shirts. I found a seat by the coach's wife. Diane said, "You look good in that pink shirt. Thanks for supporting the cause."

Then I said something and had no idea that I made a mistake.

"Yes," I said. "Anything I can do to support breast awareness." She looked at me and burst into laughter.

"Breast awareness!" she said. "You mean breast *cancer* awareness!" I flushed red. I couldn't believe I had made such a mistake. For the rest of the game, every time I thought of what I said, I chuckled. So did she.

Unfortunately, that mistake lodged in the recesses of my mind. The next time I wore the shirt, it was at a social function in downtown Erie. Someone asked me why I was wearing a pink shirt.

"For breast awareness," I replied. Round Two of embarrassment and laughter.

Round Three. That summer, Extreme Makeover: Home Edition came to Erie. It was a reality TV show that constructed new homes for families in difficult situations and in need of hope. The show's producers coordinated with a local construction contractor and with donated materials and labor, an incredible miracle would happen.

MISHAPS, MISTAKES, AND MISCHIEF

As Clara Ward's home went up in just four days, dozens of businesses and hundreds of volunteers showed up. So did hundreds of observers. It was an incredible experience to see the community come together, to see the TV crews film what would become an episode on national TV, and to see the house come to completion.

The excitement was high in town, and I decided to visit the site every day. Yes, I proudly wore my pink T-shirt one day, and someone asked me about it.

"Oh, yes," I responded. "It's for breast awareness." I froze for an awkward split second. I couldn't believe I kept making that same darn mistake! Just ask my wife; it's happened several times since. But I think I've finally got it right – breast *cancer* awareness.

Little did I think that my daughter Rachel, thirty-three years old at the time, would come down with Stage Four breast cancer. I've never been more aware of breast cancer in my life. She's responded incredibly well to treatment and we're hopeful for the future.

Even though I can't see pink, that color has a new meaning for me. Whenever I think I see a pink T-shirt, I think about the terrible disease breast cancer is. I think about the innocent mistake I used to make. And I say a prayer for somebody with breast cancer. My hope is that one day, dollars raised for research will bring about a cure.

But from now on, I'll let my pink shirt do the talking for me!

Postscript by Nancy Clark:

I was sitting in a courtroom waiting for my husband's hearing to begin. It had been beyond stressful leading up to that day. In support, Pastor Al sat on one side of me, Pastor Mike Watson on the other.

Extreme Makeover was in Erie, and Grace Church was involved. Pastor Al started telling us about visiting the work site earlier. He said, "I was wearing my breast awareness T-shirt." Pastor Mike said, "Al, I think you mean breast *cancer* awareness." Serious and clueless, Pastor

Al replied, "No, no! I meant breast awareness."

In one of my most serious of days, I laughed till I cried. Thank you, Pastor Al, I needed that!

71

BATHROOM EMERGENCIES

An elephant in the room is something that everyone knows exists, but no one wants to talk about. Bathroom emergencies is one of them. We all have emergencies. But whether because of embarrassment or inappropriateness, we rarely speak about them.

You probably won't publish *your* emergencies. But as I write about mine, you're likely to experience one of several responses – "I identify," "It's funny," "I'm glad we're all human," "A pastor would say this?" "I think I'll skip this chapter." For those of you who stay with me, here goes.

When we lived in Chicago, two couples of us went to visit another couple in our church, Don and Nancy Geske, several suburbs away. John and Karen drove. Marie and I sat in the back seat. We had a splendid evening of fun and plenty to eat.

Ready to return home, we got in the car and took off around 10:45pm. Ten minutes into our journey, I had such a bearing down that I knew I'd never make it home. I alerted John, "Get me to the nearest gas station as quick as you can!"

We drove to a Texaco station. It closed at 11:00pm. It was 10:59. A clerk was in the store. The sign said *Closed*. I couldn't take *no* for an answer, so I pounded on the door. He ignored me. I pounded some more. Finally, he came to the door.

I pled my case, but the clerk wasn't having it. Maybe he wanted to get home. Maybe he thought it was a robbery ready to happen.

I played my final card. With knees bent, I pled, "Please Mr., have mercy on me! It's gonna happen right here at your door if you don't." His hardened face softened, and he went for the key.

I scurried to the restroom. No sooner had I dropped my drawers than there was a colossal explosion. I'm sure he heard it on the other side of the wall. My life was spared and I returned the key with a relieved look on my face. The attendant received the key with an *I've done my good deed for the day* look on his face. And John and Karen? They were happy that someone had mercy on me and that their rear car seat was spared.

* * *

Years later, I was in a restaurant in Waterford, Pennsylvania. It was old and quaint with décor from years gone by. Marie and I had a wonderful dinner and, afterward, we sat chatting. Suddenly, I knew I had a bathroom emergency. I alerted Marie, "See you later!"

God answered my prayers. Not only was the toilet stall vacant, so was the men's room. I sat on the toilet as fast as I could. The outcome was the same as at the Texaco station – an explosion that would have registered on the Richter Scale.

At the same time, I heard the men's room door open. I pulled my feet up from the floor to give the impression that the stall was empty. It was too late. I have no idea who the guy was, but he must have been an extrovert with little tact. I'll always remember his words, "Hey buddy, I think you just blew up your *ss!"

I blushed in secret and didn't make a sound until he left. And then I took an extra five minutes in the bathroom hoping he wouldn't be looking to see who came out the door. Once back at the table, I told Marie my story and her sympathetic reply was, "Only among men."

Curiosity got the best of me. Surely, I couldn't be the only guy with experiences like this. I tested the waters. I'd been friends with Pastor Mike Watson, a guy on my church staff, and we could talk about anything, from the gross to the spiritual.

I told him about the explosion at the restaurant. It was comforting to hear him say, "I know exactly what you mean. I was in Walmart one day and the exact same thing happened to me. I had a bathroom emergency. The men's room was completely vacant when the explosion happened. The only problem? The smell was unbearable. Next thing I know, someone walked into the restroom and I'll never forget his words, 'Mother of God!' I also took my time exiting the restroom." Mike and I were now bathroom emergency buddies.

* * *

Lest you think this is an ongoing thing, let me put things in perspective. I've only had about four or five public emergencies in my adult life. Let me turn to the last one.

Grace Church relocated to a brand-new campus in 2007. I was Senior Pastor and had lots of friends in the neighborhood, community, and in professional settings. They didn't go to my church, but they were very interested in the relocation project. So I had a special open house for them at our new church.

The night was as nasty as you could get in early December – high winds with driving rain and sleet. A surprising number braved the elements. They loved our new facilities.

It was approaching 9:00pm when the last of the guests left. Marie and I were doing the cleanup work when I exclaimed, "You'll never guess what. I've got a bathroom emergency! I'll never make it home." And I disappeared.

When I finished my business, I stood up and turned around for the flush. But there was something odd floating in the toilet! I looked and did a double-take. It was a greeting card in its envelope.

I had totally forgotten that one of my guests had given me an oversized card. I had no place to put it and I didn't want to forget it, so I tucked it into the back waist of my pants. My belt held it in place while my sport coat covered it.

A dilemma stood before me – a card in a soiled commode. How was I to get it? I couldn't flush with it sitting in there.

A wad of paper towels saved the day as I retrieved the card and flushed the toilet. The next step was to wash the dampened envelope in the sink.

I finally opened the card. The sentiments expressed inside were exceptional and so was the contents – a damp fifty-dollar bill. The card went into the trash and the money got its needed cleansing in the sink.

I never dreamed that bathroom emergencies would lead me to money laundering.

72

THE PIANO

Far too often, churches end up with clunker pianos that take up space but are never used.

When we relocated our entire church campus, we didn't have that problem. We left the junk pianos behind.

We did, however, bring our baby grand piano to the new Worship Center, as well as an upright piano for the Commons. Turns out, we could have used a good piano or two in other parts of the new campus.

One night in our small group meeting, Gary and Diane Renaud shared, "We have friends who'd be willing to donate their piano to the church. It's a very nice upright piano. What do you think?"

I responded, "Sounds like we might be in business. Let me send one of our musicians over to their house to check it out." I'd never met their friends, but I felt incredibly blessed that they were willing to donate a piano to a church they didn't attend.

Gary and Diane love good music but they're not exactly musicians. What looks good to the untrained eye and ear may be just another clunker in disguise. So they made arrangements for someone to inspect the piano.

Out went one of our scouts. "When you're done with your visit, give me a report on what you think," I instructed. The report came back solidly positive. The piano could be donated to the church. Because that piano was better than the one in the Commons, the plan was to put the incoming piano in the Commons and find somewhere else in the church for the existing one.

We wondered how we were going to get the piano from the donor's house to the church. But the recruitment of a truck and several guys happened quickly, and all the arrangements were made. Soon the guys were on their way to the church with the piano.

My cell phone rang. It was Brian Lusky, our Worship Pastor. "We have a problem. The guys didn't secure the piano very well. And, uh, well, it fell over in the truck and it's a mess." I thought he was kidding, but the tone of his voice was dead serious.

"You've got to be kidding me! The piano only had to travel less than two miles," I lamented.

"Meet me in the Commons," said Brian. I hurried to the church. There sat the donated piano in an obvious state of agony.

"What are we going to do?" I implored.

"Let's get a piano guy to see if it's fixable and what it would cost to repair it. We'll start there," sighed Brian.

A few days later, the report came back. The piano was terminal. "Now what do we do?" queried Brian. "What do we tell the donors? And who will tell them?"

I'm thinking, *This will be an all-time low public relations moment.*

"I'll do it," I sighed. "I'll tell Gary and Diane. I'm sure they'll find a good way to break the news to the donors." But I couldn't imagine how and doubted that any of them would take the news well.

I knew I couldn't delay the inevitable. I had to get this over with – and fast. I called Gary and Diane, speaking in low tones. "I need to see you. I have something urgent to tell you. Can I come over right now?" I could tell that I had piqued their curiosity, but they didn't ask me why.

"Sure, come on over." I hung up the phone and anxiously got in my car.

All the way over, I rehearsed in my mind what I'd say. There was no way to dance around it. I had to get it off my chest immediately by telling them exactly what happened.

The three of us sat down in their comfortable living room. They leaned toward me expectantly. I could tell they were thinking, *What in the world is he going to say?*

Out it came.

"Well, you know the piano that your friends donated to the church? It fell over in the truck on the way to the church." I relayed the whole story to them.

They leaned back with a sigh of relief and started to laugh. "That's all? That's what you came over here for? We thought you were coming to tell us that you and Marie were having marital problems or that you were leaving the church or something like that. The piano? That's not a problem. Don't worry about it."

I couldn't believe their response! I relaxed and felt extremely relieved, even though I still felt awkward. But I had one big question, "Will the donors take the news this easily?"

They assured me all would be well and that they'd let me know how the donors responded. I apologized again and left their home. The next day, I got the word. All was well with the donors.

And the piano? It went to piano heaven. A new electronic keyboard went to the Worship Center. The baby grand went into the Commons. And the piano in the Commons found another home in the building.

Gary, Diane, and I still laugh about the drama of it all. And some day, I hope to meet the forgiving donors! Further, I decided that raw recruit movers probably aren't the best way to move expensive furniture.

73

THE EXPRESS CHECKOUT

E xpress checkout lanes in grocery stores test my spirituality. I walk into the store for a few items. I'm in a good mood. The lines are a little long, but that's okay. There's an express lane. Sometimes there are two express lanes open. I have two or three items, and it should be a breeze. I choose the lane I've assessed to be the quickest – which, of course, is always the wrong one. Something happens to the cash register. Something doesn't have a price. The clerk has to call a supervisor. It's too late to change lanes.

I can usually handle these kinds of slowdowns. What tests my spirituality are the people in front of me with a cartload of groceries. The well-placed sign clearly reads in bold letters, "Express Checkout – 15 Items or Less." I find it hard to believe that anyone would challenge that sign, but they do. It happens almost every time I check out.

Some of my misery is self-inflicted. I could go through the self-checkout line. There are usually four or more of them open, and there's always a clerk floating around to assist if you run into a problem.

But I'm old-fashioned. I like to put my groceries on the rolling belt. I like to see the clerk. I like them to tell me what to do with my credit card. And I like them to bag my groceries.

So, I get into an express lane. The person in front of me has a pile of groceries in his cart and a pile on the belt. I can't help myself. I feel frustration welling up within. It's almost a vigilante spirit that takes hold as I dream of telling them to pick up their excessive pile of groceries and go through the regular checkout lane.

Of course, it's all a fantasy. I never do a darn thing.

Except this. I fuel my frustration by counting. I count every item they put on the belt. If it's a six-pack, I feel like counting each can. The more I count, the more I'd like to have a conversation with the person.

My only hope is that the clerk will say something when the cart approaches the belt. All they'd have to say is, "We're so glad you've chosen to shop in our store. But this lane is for 15 items or less. Thanks for moving to another lane."

In all my years watching the clerk/customer experience in the middle of an overload violation, I've never heard a clerk object to the volume in the cart. They say absolutely nothing! They start scanning the items, and the items keep on coming.

Then one day it happened. The clerk looked at the mountain of groceries on the belt and asked, "Which 15 of these items would you like to buy?" There was a tense moment, followed by a brief stand-off, but then nothing more was said. She scanned all the items. But she still scored huge in my book. She had made her point.

There are times I end up behind a loaded cart, and my hope exceeds reality. I make my two or three items visibly obvious. I stop short of waving them in the person's face. I think to myself, *There's no way they're not going to let me go before them.*

Never happens. They ignore me like I'm not even there. It's the person who has eleven items that says to me with my three, "You have fewer groceries than I do. You can go ahead of me." But not the cart bullies. They don't budge from their territory.

This topic of the express lane came up one day at lunch with several of my church staff in New Castle, Pennsylvania. It was comforting to know that I'm not the only one who experiences the overrunning of the express lanes by people with too many items. It's good to know that my frustration is matched, even surpassed, by others.

Lloyd Lamm spoke up and out came the best story I've ever heard about this problem. It was about 11:00pm. He and his wife were on their way home when they realized they needed an item at the grocery store. Donna stayed in the car while Lloyd ran in. *People shouldn't be swamping the express lane with groceries at this time of night,* he thought. He got the item and should have been out the door quickly.

Wouldn't you know it? Lloyd got behind a lady in the express checkout lane with a cart full of groceries. It was going to be a long wait. He could feel his displeasure rising, and it came out with a laser-like stare to the back of her head. There was no way she could see it, but somehow she must have felt it. She eventually turned around and said, "What?" in a semi-confrontational way.

Lloyd has a way with words. Without a pause, he pointed to the "15 items or less" sign and responded, "Well, l was just wondering if you couldn't count or if you couldn't read." There was no reply from the lady but the clerk overheard the exchange with a subtle and subdued nod of approval.

The shopper eventually completed her mission, and off she went. Who knows what she was thinking? But the checkout clerk loved it and rewarded Lloyd.

"Your item is free!" she told him. At least there was some justice served.

People seem to enjoy this story because most of us have been there. But if you ever happen to exceed your limit at the express lane, beware of Lloyd!

74

THE UNDERPANTS

Marie and I have been hosting tours to Israel every few years since 1984. These tours touch people at many levels – spiritual, cultural, historical, social, and emotional. But it's not all a serious adventure. There's a lot of humor that bubbles to the surface. Funny things happen that overtake the group. It's to one of the funniest episodes ever that I now turn.

Baptism in the Jordan River is always a highlight. I baptize fifteen to twenty people on almost every tour. Most people wouldn't go for it if the baptism was in the States. The water is chillingly cold and murky muddy. Many people gasp as I take them down because of the cold shock, and their white robes look like they've been steeped in a large pot of tea when they emerge from the water.

We had just finished our morning baptism experience, and all of us were on the bus ready to journey to Masada, when a staff man from the baptism site approached the bus. He had a garment in his hand and said that someone had left it in the men's changing room.

At the time, I was standing in the front of the bus talking to my group. "Excuse me for a moment," I said as I reached for the garment. It was a pair of men's underpants dyed muddy brown from the Jordan River. I thought to myself, *Nobody's gonna claim these even if they belong to them!* But I asked anyway.

Midway back in the bus, a man's hand went up. Gary Weimer was a retired schoolteacher and an Elder in the church where I was the Interim Pastor. "Uh, I think those are mine." The bus erupted in laughter as I sent the garment back to its owner.

People chuckled and laughed as the subject came up from time to time throughout the day. It was good-natured banter as the underpants lay in the bus to dry out.

The touring days came and went and so did the group's memory of the underpants moment. But it didn't leave *my* mind. I tend to get mileage from things like this.

We always have a free day on our next-to-last day of the tour. People get to roam around the Old City of Jerusalem, and they have a blast. *I* was in the Old City on a mission.

You see, we end each trip with a special farewell dinner. After we eat, every person gets an award. It's an award that captures something funny or unique about each person. I wanted to buy a pair of underpants with dangling beads and fancies for Gary's award. I declined something for $46 because no fun prize is worth that much money. Marie and I searched all day and came up empty.

Not to be denied, Marie said, "Why don't you ask Gary's wife for a pair of his clean underpants? That would be even funnier." So Marie agreed to ask Marlene for a pair of Gary's underpants on one condition – he was not to know. She was more than happy to oblige.

When the meal was over, it was awards time. One by one, I said something about each person and named their award. For example, Greg and Sue Tower got the "Ballroom Dancing Award," because during a delay at the Istanbul airport, they began to gracefully dance to some live piano music.

Forty-eight awards were given out and I was down to the last one by design – Gary's. But before I gave out the award, I reached for a little plastic bag on the table and said, "Before I forget, the hotel gave me this bag and said that maybe it belonged to someone in our group. I reached into the bag and held up its contents.

Out came the underpants Gary's wife had given us. As I shook them out, I said, "Do these belong to anyone?" The place went crazy. I couldn't compose the crowd. As I held up the underpants, Gary said confidently to his wife while others listened in, "At least I know *they're* not mine!" Marlene looked at him and said, "Oh yes they are!" and his face flushed bright red.

At last, the levity subsided and I announced the final award, "And to Gary Weimer goes the Captain Underpants Award!" Once again, the crowd exploded in laughter. For the rest of the evening and the trip home, the "underpants" award was the talk of the group.

But the caper didn't end there. Once we returned home, I bought a pair of red shorts with little dangling pompoms from the hem. I had moved back full-time to Erie by then, so I called Jan Weaver, the secretary of First Baptist Church where I had served in New Castle, Pennsylvania, and where Gary was an Elder. I asked if she'd be my partner in crime. I explained the situation and inquired, "If I mail those shorts to you, will you secretly get them to Gary's wife? Have her wrap them and put them under their Christmas tree from his 'Secret Santa.'" All was arranged.

Christmas Eve came, and I could hardly stand the anticipation: *When will Gary open his gifts? What will be his reaction when he sees those shorts?* I wished I could have been a mouse. At 9:10pm, my text prompt sounded. Could it be Gary?

It was! In a picture without text, Gary was in his red shorts with a frown on his face.

Mission accomplished!

I've been in touch with Gary several times since then. Invariably the subject of the underpants comes up and we laugh. The story keeps spreading. It's become an urban legend.

And the moral of the story? If you ever leave your underpants behind, never admit they're yours!

75

THE TOP CANDIDATE

My office phone rang in February of 2013. It was a familiar voice on the other end of the line – the Executive Minister of our district, Dan Peterson. His voice was familiar, but his question was not.

Would I ever consider doing interim pastoring?

I had been at Grace Church in Erie, Pennsylvania, for nearly 35 years, 32 years as Senior Pastor and, following that, nearly three as an Associate Pastor. My plans were to retire from Grace sometime in my 70s.

I didn't give Dan an overly optimistic answer, but I said something all Christians recognize as somewhat dangerous: "I'll pray about it."

Before I knew it, I left Grace Church and became the Interim Pastor at Old North Church in Canfield, Ohio. I spent nearly two years there. Pastor Nick Gatzke was a great hire following me.

After that, First Baptist Church in New Castle, Pennsylvania, beckoned. I spent two years and four months there, until they called the very capable Pastor Mike Willmer as Lead Pastor.

A call from Christ Community Church in Fredonia, New York, followed a hiatus of nine months. I spent a total of twenty-one months there. Pastor Josh Stahley was called, and he began to ignite excitement. All three churches belonged to our denomination, Converge MidAtlantic.

As an intentional interim pastor, my major job is to preach the Word, catalyze the leadership, work on weaknesses in the church, and facilitate a smooth transition to a permanent pastor. My goal is always to turn over a church buzzing and ready to move forward into a bright future.

The Search Teams worked hard in each church. I served as a consultant to them but stayed out of any matters that would influence their decision concerning who their final pastoral candidate would be. Of course, as the Team neared the "finish line," I was apprised of the finalists and asked to interview them. I'd give the Team my report, and they could factor it in any way they'd choose.

The choice of the final candidates in the first two churches went exceptionally well. I expected the same at Christ Community Church.

Daryl Brautigam, the chair of the Search Team and a key founding member of the church, kept me up-to-date about the general progress of the search. "We have some pretty sharp and solid candidates. The Team and I are very excited!" Things were moving along more rapidly than I had expected. But I was told little about the specifics.

One afternoon, I was at home in Erie working in my office when I got an email from Daryl. The subject line said, "Sneak peek." The subject? "Our top guy so far." With it was a YouTube link to one of his sermons.

Up to this point, I hadn't had *any* sneak peeks for *any* candidate, so I was a little surprised. But Daryl is a good leader, and I thought he must want to run this exciting "leader of the pack" by me. He and the Team had been so excited about this emerging secret top guy.

Immediately I went to the link, ready to feast on the sermon that had taken Daryl and the Team by storm. I wasn't ready for what I saw. It was legalistic preaching. Awkward body movements. Bad vocal mannerisms. Contortions of the face. Quite frankly, a total turnoff.

Instantly, I began to sweat and feel sick to my stomach. I had spent quality time with the Team. I had coached them. I was sure they could be trusted to evaluate good preaching. My mind raced: *This is their top guy?! What went wrong? How could my influence lead to this?*

I bolted up the stairs to voice my consternation to Marie. "You won't believe what you're about to see! Please come immediately to my office."

I showed her the email and then took her to the link. Within three minutes, she was as sick as I was. If this guy were called to the church, well, you might as well write its obituary.

Marie and I kept shaking our heads and commenting to each other about the incredulity of it all.

About an hour later, when Marie called me for dinner, I still couldn't shake my disappointment. *How could this happen? Am I in the Twilight Zone?* I barely had any appetite.

But something began to dawn on me as I ate my dinner. "What's today's date?" I queried. "April 1," Marie replied.

I shouted, "It's April Fools Day and I've just been had!" Relief flooded me as I felt confidence in Daryl and the Search Team begin to rebound.

I bolted to my computer and replied to Daryl, "I don't think he should be your top dog. But you should definitely consider him as an associate pastor." By this, he'd know that I was on to him. Then I added, "Look out for paybacks!"

He responded, "Right now the laughter is a welcome respite from all the Covid news. Thanks for going along and not getting irritated!" Some of his friends had been worried about my reaction.

That evening, when we chatted on the phone, I gave Daryl my play-by-play, downward spiral of disbelief and how, all of a sudden, it had dawned on me that I had been pranked. He could hardly contain his laughter as his gratification of success hemorrhaged through. I went to bed that night relieved yet amazed that I had so thoroughly taken the bait.

Oh, Daryl! Paybacks are coming!

76

THE TOASTER

Interim pastoral ministry was an unexpected, but God-planned, adventure for me. I was in uncharted territory when Old North Church called me to fill my first interim pastorate.

The leaders in the Canfield, Ohio, church had plans to put me into a nice, comfortable apartment. My weekly rhythm would be roughly four days in Canfield and three at home in Erie, Pennsylvania. But the apartment they found for me fell through.

Not far from the church was an older, little white house. It wasn't nearly as nice as the apartment, but it was fine for a temporary ministry. Being an older home, it had its array of little problems, but nothing formidable.

The biggest issue was the water. It was good old Ohio well water and that meant a high level of sulfur. Anyone who knows about sulfur in the water knows that it smells like rotten eggs, and it isn't very pleasant to drink. I solved the drinking problem with bottled water. But I had this strange aroma around me after a shower.

Turns out, there was another problem, a largely invisible problem – furry, little creatures called mice. I never saw them, but they left their little collections on many surfaces to let me know we were roommates.

Traps with peanut butter were somewhat successful in controlling the population.

My wife came to stay with me most weekends. Of course, the house had telltale signs of a bachelor's residence. Marie would often clean and spruce up the place, for which I was most grateful.

Cooking meals wasn't my specialty, so the toaster became one of my major cooking companions in the morning. The entrees ranged from toast to frozen waffles to bagels. Amish maple syrup with whipped cream draping the waffles was a great launch to the day and quite a regular occurrence.

One weekend, Marie's cleaning endeavors brought her to the kitchen counter top. She started to clean it when she announced, "Hate to tell you this, but you have company."

"What do you mean?" I replied.

"Well, there are mouse droppings behind the toaster." It wasn't the kind of news I wanted to hear, but I could get past it.

Shortly thereafter came another announcement. "You're not going to like this one bit either, but there are mouse droppings in the bottom of your toaster." My blood ran cold!

I thought about the many mornings I had used the toaster with such delight and confidence. Now, all I could visualize was mice sneaking into the slot of my toaster, their furry bodies slithering down the toaster side-wires and depositing their business on the bottom after faring sumptuously on the crumbs. My stomach lurched.

Try as I might, I couldn't get that image out of my mind – mice frolicking in my toaster and leaving their evidence behind – evidence only visible to the one who cleaned it. The idea was revolting.

Since the toaster was almost new, Marie volunteered, "Tell you what I'm gonna do. I'll thoroughly clean and disinfect it and you'll be back in business in no time."

Soon the toaster sat on the counter top once again sparkling like new.

But every time I saw that toaster, I cringed. I couldn't imagine putting another frozen waffle or slice of bread into its belly.

I posted on Facebook and confessed that all these goings on had traumatized me. I called it "PTMS" – *Post Traumatic Mouse Syndrome*. The "likes" and humorous comments on Facebook ran in the dozens.

But I just couldn't get past that toaster. One day I determined it had to go. I explained the psychological aspects involved in making such a decision to Marie. She was sympathetic and supported my throwing out a perfectly good toaster, if it would calm me down.

Soon the offending toaster was out the door and into the trash. It was cathartic and I felt better almost instantly. Then we headed off to *Bath, Bed, and Beyond* for a new one. Incredibly, I bought the same model. I knew I had to get past my phobia.

The new toaster found a home in the same spot on the counter top. But this time, it resided under a toaster cover complete with a heavy plate on top of it for insurance. I could hardly bring myself to use it the first time. But I got past it, even though images of mice in my toaster danced in my head with every waffle bite I took.

I checked that toaster thoroughly before each use. There were no more mouse intrusions for the rest of my stay in that house. But I still bear the scars of mouse images every time I use a toaster.

I'll never fully trust one again.

III

Overheard

Humorous stories told in my presence.

77

THE BODY SHOP

When I was a student at the Moody Bible Institute in the 1960's, there were some notable class comedians. Two of them were Fenton McDonald and Glenn Kehrein. That funny duo brought us to laughter and tears multiple times.

After graduation, people move on. I found myself surrounded by new friends and new class comedians at Dallas Theological Seminary. Lord knows, we needed comedic relief in the hallowed halls of sacred higher education. I lost track of Fenton and Glenn.

One of the ways we don't lose total track of distant friends is when something is featured about them in the school's alumni publications. We see births, marriages, books written, ministry updates and, yes, deaths. In 2011, it was hard to see Glenn's name listed among those who were called home to be with the Lord. He had a significant ministry and ran his race well.

The clock kept ticking and soon our 50th anniversary of graduation and reunion was upon us. Nearly 40 of us gathered with spouses and other relatives on the hallowed grounds of the school that D. L. Moody founded. Miracle of miracles, most of us were able to recognize each other.

In one of our reunion meetings, we were all given several minutes to share. People talked about their last 50 years – from highs to lows, from accomplishments to losses, from jobs to family. It was both riveting and draining to hear all the stories.

Halfway through the chain of sharing, it was Fenton's turn. The big question on everyone's mind was – did life take away his gift of comedy and laughter? Would he still hold the unofficial title of class comedian?

In just a second or two, we had our answer. His first few sentences drew forth laughter. It never stopped until he sat down.

In the course of sharing, Fenton told the following story. He wrote what follows specifically for this chapter. Join the Class of '69 in laughter.

I had a job at a mortuary while attending seminary. Here's how it came about.

I called my wife about a job offer. I told her that it was an offer to work in a body shop and that it had a great benefit – we'd be able to live above it rent-free. I sensed that she wasn't thrilled with the idea when she informed me that she didn't want to live above an old smelly, greasy, noisy auto repair shop.

I told her it wasn't that kind of body shop.

"I think where you grew up, they're called mortuaries," I replied. She was even less thrilled when she heard this, but she finally agreed and we moved above the mortuary.

Part of my job was to pick up the remains of loved ones who had passed away. One Saturday, while working a funeral, the director called me aside and said that someone had passed away at a nursing home. He asked me to retrieve the body. Then he added, "Be sure to comfort the wife and family, because they'll be fragile with the sudden passing of their loved one."

Off I went to the nursing home in the first-call car. I arrived, unloaded the rolling cot, and entered the facility. When I got to the room, the wife was being supported by her daughter on one side and her son-in-law on the other. I offered my condolences and told them to take whatever time they needed. They could come to the mortuary the next day to make arrangements. About that time a nurse approached me with a sense of urgency, motioning me to follow her. She whispered that someone had died.

We entered another room. A man was in the bed and the nurse informed me that they couldn't find his dentures. They knew we'd want them to set the facial features. She started going through drawers and finally said that she didn't know if they were in his mouth.

Well, the one sure way to find out is to stick your fingers into the mouth.

I walked over to the deceased and, with my two index fingers a couple of inches apart, I pointed them downward. As my hand descended, at the very last moment, he opened his eyes. I could feel my heart stop! Frozen in place, I stood there with both index fingers an inch from his mouth.

"Hello," he said. Stunned, I tried to say hello back but could hardly get the word out.

Turning from him and waiting for my heart to start beating again, I made my way to the door. The family of the "deceased" was looking into the room, inquiring if everything was okay. I managed to squeak out, "Oh, everything is just fine." It was then I realized the nurse had taken me to the wrong room. The actual deceased was indeed in the room next door, where I had been.

I quickly moved the truly deceased to my rolling cot and placed him in the first-call car to take him back to the mortuary. When I arrived and placed him on the embalming table, the funeral director looked at me and exclaimed, "What's wrong with you? You're white as a sheet and look like you've just seen a ghost."

For a moment, I honestly thought I had.

78

THE TRIAL

When I was Interim Pastor at Old North Church in Canfield, Ohio, it was a pleasure to work with the Elder Board. They were men of God and a group that bonded well together. They were serious about the well-being of the church. We met at least twice a month. One meeting was the formal meeting, complete with an agenda. The other was a 6:30am continental breakfast with our focus on a topic of discussion or a book. The Pastoral Staff joined in on this one.

For sure, no meeting would slip by without a funny moment or two. Tom Gacse, an attorney, made sure of that. He always had a smile on his face and a humorous story. One night, his story stole the show. It was an attorney story as only he could tell it. It went like this:

One night a shooting occurred at the County Line Bar. I was the prosecutor assigned to the Felonious Assault case. Fortunately, there was an eyewitness to the shooting. The case seemed simple enough; two men seated at the bar got into a heated argument and one of them pulled out a gun and shot the other. The eyewitness was seated next to them and observed the whole thing.

I met with the eyewitness on the day of the trial to prepare him and go over his testimony. We covered all the details of the shooting. The witness explained how he observed the two men arguing and saw the defendant pull out his gun and shoot the other man. He assured me that he was prepared and ready to testify.

The trial began. After opening statements by the attorneys, it was time for the prosecution to present its case. I called my eyewitness to the stand. With his left hand on the Bible, he swore to tell the truth, the whole truth, and nothing but the truth, so help me God.

I would soon find out that this witness took his oath literally and very seriously.

Following a few preliminary questions, I asked, "Did you have an occasion to be at the County Line Bar on the evening of September 7 between the hours of 9 and 11:00pm?"

"No," said the eyewitness with a straight face, looking me squarely in the eyes. I was totally startled and began to check if I had given the correct date and time. I did.

Maybe somehow, the eyewitness had misunderstood the question. So I rephrased it slightly. "Did you have an occasion to be in the County Line Bar on a night in September and, while sitting at the bar, witness an argument between two men?"

Again, with a straight face, looking me squarely in the eyes, the witness emphatically said, "NO!"

Now I was at a total loss. I assumed that someone had talked this witness into changing his story. I was ready to ask the Judge to declare him as a hostile witness, but decided to give the questioning one more try.

"Let me ask you something, sir," I spoke emphatically to the testifier. "Do you recall our discussion in the hallway, prior to you testifying today?"

"Yes, I do," the witness replied.

I continued with my questioning. "Do you recall us discussing a shooting that you observed at the County Line Bar?

"Yes," stated the witness again, looking me squarely in the eyes without

changing his expression.

"Did you or did you not tell me that you were sitting at the bar and observed the Defendant shoot the other man?"

"I did," the witness replied emphatically.

Exasperated, I continued my questioning. "Then why on earth do you keep answering No when I ask you if you had an occasion to be there at that time and witness the shooting?"

The witness, looking very seriously at me, replied, "I took an oath to tell the whole truth. When you asked if I had an occasion to be at the bar that night, I had to be honest. There was no occasion for me to be there. I just wanted a drink."

I shook my head and grinned. The courtroom erupted in laughter. Even the judge was smiling!

At that point, I changed my line of questioning with the witness, leaving out whether the witness had an occasion to be in the bar, and the proceedings concluded without a hitch.

I won the case. But when I think of the witness's response to the "occasion" question, I still shake my head and laugh. And whenever I have an occasion to tell the story, everyone laughs as well.

It's become a laughter classic.

79

THE PUMPKIN CANNON

I t's been my experience that on every Elder Board I've been part of, there's one guy who stands out in the humor department. Usually it's an ever-present, dry sense of humor. The Elder Board at First Baptist Church in New Castle, Pennsylvania, was no exception.

When I interviewed for the position of Interim Pastor at the church, the interview team was comprised of three Elders. We met at a restaurant for lunch. Instantly, we sensed chemistry. And I could see the humor bubbling out of Dr. Jim Snow. He was also a dentist, who soon became mine. With his sense of humor, he made dentistry fun. And Elders' meetings, as well.

At one of our meetings, Jim told the following story. We laughed the whole way through. In his own words:

One fall, our church decided to have a "Fall Festival." As part of the festival, members were invited to invent and fabricate pumpkin hurling machines. It was going to be a contest. I was all in.

Off to YouTube I went to research my design. I settled on a giant potato cannon that would be charged with compressed air. The breach of my cannon would be a cylinder of Schedule 40 PVC. This "Air Tank" and a giant quick release valve would loosen the compressed air behind the pumpkin, shooting it out of the PVC barrel.

Fearful that the tank might explode after charging, I filled the tank with water and charged it to twice the pressure I intended to use. It held just fine. I noted that the rated pressure for this pipe was way over my target charging capability. However, the rated pressure had one important qualification – "maximum working pressure 180 psi at 73° F."

The cannon was a huge hit, and I took the blue ribbon. Kids were lining up to discharge the weapon. We blew an air horn to announce the next firing. One of our members recorded a video for a couple of launches and sent me a copy. I shared it on Facebook so my friends could enjoy my success.

As a result of my enthusiastic distribution of the video, I was contacted by a pastor friend who was very interested in me bringing my device to his church's "Fall Festival." How could I resist being the star of yet another show? In preparation, I collected about twenty 6" pumpkins from a local purveyor at a very good price, since it was for a good cause "in the service of the Lord." Once home, a young friend and I washed the pumpkins to prep them for the event.

At this point I must explain that the temperature on the day of this "Fall Festival" was quite nippy, well below 73° F. I was wearing long pants and a hoodie.

I knew the festival was supposed to last 2 hours. I became concerned that I might not have enough pumpkins. To determine how many I would need, I had to know how long the "air tank" would take to fully recharge.

We had already loaded the cannon into the back of my Suburban, so I figured that we would just charge it there and see how long it took. I plugged the compressor into the tank and turned it on. The maximum pressure of the compressor was set to my desired final charging pressure, about 90 psi.

I was standing by the right rear passenger door. My young helper, Zach, was at the left rear door. As we got almost to maximum pressure, I heard a slight cracking sound and advised Zach to get away from the vehicle. A second slightly softer "crack" sounded and I stepped behind the roof support pillar on my side of the SUV. As soon as I did there was a tremendous explosion. I feared I had killed Zach.

I looked to see if he was okay. The window in that door was gone. I couldn't see him. I ran around the vehicle and, to my amazement and relief, he was unscathed. A miracle!! I was okay, too. Another miracle!

The PVC had shot out of the side and rear doors. Jagged shards of white PVC were everywhere. An eighty foot circle around the vehicle was littered with cannon parts. The rear AC controls were hanging out of the ceiling of the Suburban. The upholstery was shredded in spots from the floor to the ceiling, and a rear speaker housing and speaker were pierced.

And, there was a large convex dent in the roof. It looked like a bomb had exploded in the Suburban, without the charred remains. It was the demise of the "M1 Punkin' Chunkin' MoSheen."

No insurer would be called; the explanation would likely have raised my premiums. After my body shop man repaired the interior, he wanted to know how we got an "outie" on the roof. Sparing him the gory details I said, "Please just paint it so it doesn't rust. It was a miracle from God."

Needless to say, I had to disappoint my pastor friend and my fans, but Zach will never forget my performance. Neither will his mother, one of my dental assistants. She knew about it before I could call her to pick him up.

I never saw her text from Zach. I can only imagine what she said.

80

THE PUN-OFF

When my son Jared, a psychologist, lived in California with his family, part of our conversations included catching up on the funny side of life – his and mine. Proverbs talks about laughter being a good medicine, and we took quite a bit of it. It provided welcome relief from the stress we both felt in our professional lives.

On one of our trips, he told the following story. In my mind's eye, I could vividly see it happening, as though it were on a large-screen TV. I asked Jared to tell the story for this book. Here goes:

Sometimes funny situations are the byproduct of someone else's good intentions. This story is an example of that.

To set the stage, I was working as a civilian contractor on an Air Force base. I was a psychologist in the Mental Health Clinic, where one of the providers had reached out to a local organization called Flag Is Up Farms. The only thing I knew about them was that they had a program for veterans that involved working with horses. My colleague, Captain Seri, thought it would be a good gesture to bring them in to talk to us about the work they did with struggling veterans. Perhaps we could be a source of referrals to them. We learned later that Flag Is Up Farms is an extremely well-regarded program founded by world-famous Monte Roberts, a consultant to Queen Elizabeth II.

That morning, Major Gross, our Flight Commander, met with us to remind us about the event coming up later in the day. It's probably important to note that Major Gross has a playful streak, and he was making horse puns that morning when reminding us about the meeting.

In the midst of his punning, he struck upon an idea and threw out a challenge to the rest of us. He proposed having a secret competition (secret from the two Flag Is Up Farms staff members) to see who could make the most horse puns during the meeting without the two staff members picking up on the joke. The challenge just hung out there in the air, making it clear that only time would tell if anyone would join in with Major Gross in a pun-off that afternoon.

I was in a bit of a mental quandary about the challenge because there are two distinct parts of my personality. One is very respectful and most comfortable following the rules. The other is a childish, mischievous streak that lurks just below my calm, stoic demeanor. I spent much of the morning battling between my two sides, trying to decide which way to go.

In the end, there was one thought that made up my mind. I knew that since Major Gross threw out the challenge, he was also going to throw out at least one horse pun. I also knew that most of the rest of the flight members would be too bashful to participate. That meant all it would take is one single, solitary pun and Major Gross would win the challenge.

Did I say that there are two distinct parts of my personality? I guess I should mention a third – I'm also quite competitive. I couldn't let Major Gross claim his victory so cheaply. My competitive side conspired with my mischievous side. Knowing that I'd possibly be standing alone as Major Gross's sole challenger, the decision became easier.

Challenge him I would.

The afternoon rolled around, and our two unwitting victims showed up to give their presentation. Part of me felt badly that these well-meaning, earnest individuals were about to unknowingly be subjected to a punning competition at their horses' expense. I briefly felt conscience-stricken enough that I considered pulling out of the competition.

That is, until Major Gross dropped his first pun.

"So, is there some criteria you use with veterans to know if they're **"stable"** enough to participate in your mental health programs?"

I looked around the room to gauge the reactions of my peers. I could see that they recognized the game had begun. I was considering my options for participation when he threw down the gauntlet with a second pun.

"I bet when these veterans hear about your program, they're **"chomping at the bit"** to get started working with you."

The presenters seemed clueless.

At that point, all my resolve to be the mature adult and abstain from this game disappeared. To make matters worse, my strait-laced colleague, Capt. Davidiuk, joined in the game (although the pun was so weak that most of us didn't know at the time that he was making one): "How many people do you have on your **"team"** at the Farms?"

I "galloped" into the fray, no turning back.

"So, I understand that you're also working with troubled youth. Do these children come on their own or are they **"corralled"** from community programs?"

I noticed some strain on my colleagues' faces after this pun, as none of them wanted to break composure. A few moments later I chimed in again.

"The animal-based therapy programs are relatively new to the mental health scene, and I'm sure not all professionals are accepting of these new ideas. How do you respond to the **"nay"** sayers?"

At this point, one of my colleagues quickly left the room and didn't return. Several others coughed to hide their chuckles, as they understood why she was leaving. She was about to break.

Major Gross knew at this point that he had some serious competition, so he *threw down another pun.*

*"Going back to your youth programs, do you feel like the kids are there just to "**horse**" around, or do they participate seriously in the activities?"*

Now I was down three to two, and time was running out. I knew I had to pull out at least one more pun, when I hit upon another one.

*"Are there certain criteria that you're looking for with the participants in your veterans' programs? What I want to be careful about is not putting the "**cart before the horse**," inviting just anyone to attend if there's a certain population that you're looking for."*

At that moment I made eye contact with Major Gross. (Eye contact was essential.) He got up and fled the room abruptly. I knew that I had vanquished my foe. He had exited the battlefield. The innocent staff members wrapped up their presentation, and we thanked them for coming. Major Gross returned to the room and walked them to the front door, also thanking them for their time.

Upon his return, the room erupted in "unbridled" laughter, and Major Gross put it to a vote to see who had won the pun-off. Although he and I had thrown out the same number of puns, I had sent two people from the room in laughter. The vote was unanimous. I stood alone and victorious as the best at punning with a straight face.

I had "whipped" my challenger!

About the Author

Al Detter has been involved in the church his entire life. His journey includes the following in chronological order: Mennonite, Brethren in Christ, Independent, Presbyterian, and Baptist. Since 1975, he has been affiliated with Converge, formerly the Baptist General Conference. His church experiences have inspired much of the material for this book.

Al grew up in Souderton, Pennsylvania. His college years took him to Moody Bible Institute (B.A.) in Chicago, Illinois, and the University of Illinois Chicago Circle Campus. He went on to Dallas Theological Seminary (Th.M.) in Dallas, Texas, and Trinity Evangelical Divinity School (D.Min.) in Deerfield, Illinois.

Al met Marie Simmons, from Peoria, Illinois, at Moody. They married in 1970. They have four grown children, three adopted as infants. They have eight grandchildren.

Al has served the following churches: Skokie Valley Baptist Church, Wilmette, IL (Youth Pastor); Grace Church, Erie, PA (35 total years, 32 as Senior Pastor); Old North Church, Canfield, OH (Interim); First Baptist Church, New Castle, PA (Interim); Christ Community Church, Fredonia, NY (Interim), and Bethel Baptist Church, Jamestown, NY (Interim).

His favorite hobbies include traveling (especially to Israel and the UK), collecting and reading antique books, and driving his 1969 Camaro.

Since laughter is a good medicine, he tries to take a good dose every day.